P9-DWA-157

DATE DUE

AP 19 '96			
FE 14 '97			
MR 29 '99			
AP 2 '99			
NO 21 '01			

Demco, Inc. 38-293

This Book is Dedicated
To the Memory of
My Sister-In-Law
and Frequent Tandem Companion
Wendy Kely Bandish
August 19, 1959 to August 8, 1988

MOUNTAIN BICYCLING

AROUND LOS ANGELES

ROBERT IMMLER

Wilderness Press
Berkeley

Copyright © 1990 by Robert Immler
Photos by the author
Design by Thomas Winnett
Cover Design by Sarah Levin
Maps by Stephen J. Eldred

Library of Congress Card Catalog Number 90-37469
International Standard Book Number 0-89997-109-1

Manufactured in the United States of America

Published by Wilderness Press
     2440 Bancroft Way
     Berkeley, CA 94704

     (415) 843-8080

     Write for free catalog

Library of Congress Cataloging-in-Publication Data

Immler, Robert.
 Mountain Bicycling around Los Angeles / Robert Immler. — 1st ed.
 p. cm.
 Includes bibliographical references (p.).
 ISBN 0-89997-109-1
 1. All terrain cycling—California—Los Angeles Metropolitan Area—Guide-books.
2. Los Angeles Metropolitan Area (Calif.)—Description and travel—Guidebooks. I. Title.
GV1045.5.C22L675 1990
796.6 ' 09794 ' 94—dc20   90-37469
                 CIP

Contents

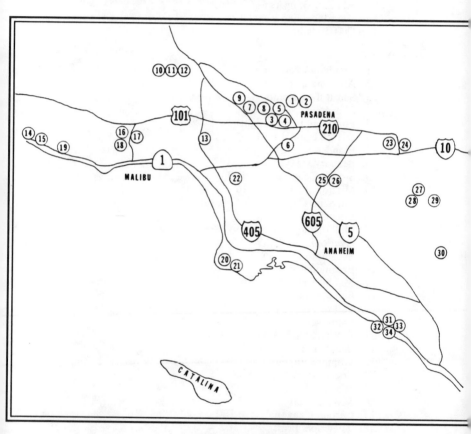

LOCATION MAP
for rides in this book

Introduction

Mountain bicycling in Los Angeles? At first thought, the two don't seem to go together. My bedroom window gives me a view of the San Gabriel Mountains first thing every morning, so it was the San Gabriels that first came to mind when mountain bicycles arrived in Los Angeles. However, on a clear day, especially from a peak in the San Gabriels, one can see that Los Angeles (particularly if you expand its definition to include sections of Orange, San Bernardino, and Ventura counties) includes many areas perfect for exploration by the mountain bicycle: the San Rafael Hills, the Verdugos, the Santa Susanas, the Santa Monicas, Palos Verdes, the Baldwin Hills, the Puddingstone Hills, the Chino Hills, and Santiago Peak, among others.

Origins of the Mountain Bike

I have always loved the mountains, so when I took up cycling, I naturally began to ride in them, first in the San Gabriels and then in the Santa Monicas. Initially, my mindset did not include the possibility of cycling in the mountains on dirt roads. I had ridden short distances on dirt roads on a conventional 10-speed, but it was always a "walking on a tightrope" experience. On dirt, the bike never felt comfortable. Then I learned of one cyclist who had gone up the Mt. Wilson Toll Road on a road bike, but even he had returned from the top on the paved Angeles Crest Highway. And I also met another cyclist who had pedaled up the Angeles Crest Highway on a heavy (steel fenders, and lights) 3-speed, and then had gone down the Toll Road. It was these two cyclists who made me realize the possibility of riding both up and downhill on the dirt roads of the mountains . . . if the appropriate bicycle were available.

1

In the mid-1970's a second bike boom was underway (the first had occurred during the Gay 90s). And although lightweight, multi-geared European bikes were popular, the restoration of 1930–1950 era American bikes, notably Schwinn "Excelsiors," introduced in 1933 by Ignaz Schwinn, became a fad. One result was the manufacturing of a modern copy of these Schwinns. But their single speeds limited them to flat terrain, and earned them the names "beach cruisers" and "klunkers."

Another group, in California's Marin county, north of San Francisco, began riding motorcycles up and down the steep slopes of Mount Tamalpais. But officials of the Marin Municipal Water District didn't like the erosion they created and outlawed the motorcycles.

Therefore, instead of using motorcycles, people soon began trucking old Schwinns and their modern imitations to the tops of the hills and riding them down the fireroads. But the coaster brakes and even the bearings were not up to the challenge. One steep route generated so much heat that the bearings had to be frequently repacked. Because of this, the route became known as the "Repack."

Gradually, people began converting these klunkers into five-speeds, Then someone made a copy of an old bike, but used modern, lightweight European bicycle tubing. To this frame, they added lightweight aluminum wheels with knobby tires, ultra-low gearing developed for touring, brakes developed for tandem bicycles, and lighter copies of motorcycle handlebars and controls.

The result: A bike that because of interest in cruisers and old bikes looked right. A bike that because of its upright handlebars was more comfortable for those who found the dropped handlebars to be backbreaking. A bike whose tires allowed it to be ridden on dirt. A bike whose brakes allowed it to be ridden downhill for miles with the calipers applied. And a bike whose gearing allowed it to be ridden uphill.

Then, sensing that a mass market existed for a bike like this, a San Jose businessman had a frame builder design a bike that could be mass produced. He named his company "Specialized" and had the frames built in Japan and Taiwan. In 1982 he introduced the first mass-market mountain bike, the Stumpjumper, for $750.

Today, there are tandem mountain bikes, mountain bikes for children, aluminum mountain bikes, mountain bikes with dropped bars, aero bars for mountain bikes, and even slick tires for the city. I've even seen, in an apparent attempt to get more traction, a mountain bike with dual rear wheels. Unfortunately, there are also fat-tired mountain bike look-a-likes sold in discount and department stores.

For me, the mountain bicycle combines the best of the two worlds of cycling and hiking. It allows me to see the same beautiful country as the hiker, but its greater efficiency allows me to enjoy about twice as much scenery in the same amount of time.

And I'm not the only one who likes mountain bikes. By 1984 they were accounting for one out of every three adult bicycles sold, and today more than 7.5 million Americans (40% more than a year ago) own mountain bikes. Amazingly, most surveys show about 80% of those mountain bikes are never ridden off pavement.

Today there are over one million bicycle riders in Southern California, and the owner of a major chain of stores in the Southland says 80% of his sales are mountain bikes. There are also at least 3 national mountain-bike magazines, and national and local mountain-bike clubs.

What's so special about mountain biking? One local cyclist states that "In just a few minutes from the city you can be out riding with red-tailed hawks, deer, wildflowers, and not see a soul; or if you do, it'll be one of like mind who's up there for the same reasons you are."

Casey Patterson, the women's winner of the 1987 Race Across America, likes to mountain bike with her children. "I can take the kids out on mountain bikes and not have to worry about them mixing with cars and trucks, plus, whether I'm riding with the kids or with a friend, we can ride two or three abreast and chat while we ride. You can't do that on the road."

Comparing road and off-road cycling, Chuck Slack-Elliott, writing in *Bicycling,* says that mountain bicycling offers ". . . rarely photographed vistas and encounters with wildlife and history unmatched on most stretches of paved roads."

Mountain bikes are also known as ATB's, or all-terrain bikes, because they're almost as much at home on the pavement as off. Only the higher rolling resistance of their knobby tires, the poorer aerodynamics of the rider's upright position, and their slightly greater weight combine to make them a little less efficient on the road than their road-racing cousins. But they make up for this by being easily able to take to the shoulder when a car decides to pass . . . just as the road narrows!

Also because they're equally at home on the pavement, they eliminate the need for a car shuttle. They can turn a tough, all-day hike requiring two cars, into a half-day bike ride, requiring only one car, if any.

Legality

Has the mountain bicycle been welcomed into the wilderness? In a word, NO!

The Sierra Club's magazine points out that "in Los Angeles, the wide-open trails of Griffith Park have been declared off-limits to bicycles. In Marin County, the Municipal Water District has closed all single-track trails to bikes. In Santa Barbara County, a popular trail in Rattlesnake Canyon has been closed in spite of a Los Padres National Forest study favoring bikes."

Can the bicycle be legally ridden on hiking trails?

Bicycling is definitely illegal in wilderness areas, and a few years ago, the bicycle was almost banned from all National Scenic Trails at the Federal level.

Signs prohibiting off-road vehicles are common. Now, the mountain bicycle is definitely a vehicle, and it is designed to be ridden off road. But these signs were erected either before mountain bicycles existed or by agencies that do not consider bicycles to be vehicles. Therefore, rangers say these signs do not apply.

But even where bicycling on trails is legal, should you ride there?

The bicycling community is divided on this issue. Charles Kelly, writing in *Bicycling*, says that if you're on a trail ". . . you go slowly, making sure that you do not skid. Your tires smoothly glide over the ground. This way, you have less impact on the earth underneath than a hiker has."

The logic behind this idea is that the fat tires of the mountain bike have a surface area equal to or greater than that of two hiking boots. Therefore, the impact of the cyclist is the same as or less than the impact of the hiker.

But I have found that in many conditions it is impossible to ride on trails without skidding a wheel. (One could argue that if the trail is steep enough you can't help but slip, even when hiking). Therefore, when I meet such conditions, either up or downhill, where my skidding wheel would erode the trail, I dismount.

Others feel that even this practice is not enough. Also writing in *Bicycling,* William Saunders says that we should not ". . . ride bicycles on hiking trails. Bike tires cut and erode the surface and cause it to wash out, a problem with which backpackers have had enough trouble without contributions by cyclists. Do not ride a bike over any sort of easily eroded surface or anywhere in a truly wild area. Stay on dirt roads . . . power-line cuts and other tracks where man already has made an ineradicable impact.

One regional park manager says the problem with bikes is they take shortcuts and make more new trails than hikers and equestrians do.

From my point of view, although the sound of knobby tires going over a leaf-covered surface is wonderful, I usually prefer to hike on trails and to ride on fireroads.

It surprised me that the first conflict regarding the bicycle in the mountains was not between cyclists and hikers, but between cyclists and equestrians. A reason for this conflict could be that the horse may recognize the cyclist not as a human but as some strange animal. Many people recommend that the cyclist, not only out of common courtesy but also for the safety of both the rider and the cyclist, stop and dismount, or at least stop, until the horse is past.

I've never had a problem with horses when I've slowed to a crawl. And once, after being given permission, I safely passed a police posse of about 30 riders. Ironically, I've had both Cleveland and Angeles National Forest rangers tell me that they felt mountain bicycles were less damaging to trails than horses.

Although it's *legal* to cycle most trails, the *morality* of cycling on trails is debatable. It appears that in the future it may become illegal to cycle not only on trails but also on some fireroads.

Griffith Park, the largest city park in the country, offers a good example of what can happen. For years, its paved roads attracted both casual riders out for a day in the park and professional riders out for a serious workout. When mountain bikes appeared, the park's fireroads and trails seemed an obvious place to ride. Unfortunately today, mountain bikes are completely banned not only from its narrow hiking trails but also from its wide fireroads.

Says one local cyclist, "The trails in Griffith Park must be 15 to 20 feet wide," a width that "precludes scaring or surprising people." Yet he is certain the decision to close them was based on "bad press" rather than facts.

Where bikes are outlawed, some cyclists ride anyway, figuring that they will not be noticed by the understaffed agencies, especially during times of little use, such as early in the morning. Not so, states an article entitled "Vicious Cycles" in an issue of *Sierra,* the national magazine of the Sierra Club. It says rangers have gotten up before dawn to give illegal cyclists $250 tickets.

According to writer Dennis Coello, when mountain bikes first appeared on the trails of Mt. Tamalpais, almost 15 years ago, "part of the thrill was the cat-and-mouse game riders played with the state-park and water-district rangers there. Today bikes are prohibited from footpaths and the area has a 15-mile-per-hour speed limit (5 mph on blind curves and when passing walkers) . . ."

The Marin Water District imposes $75 fines on cyclists who disobey the posted 15 mph limit and uses radar guns to catch them. To combat this, the *Wall Street Journal,* in a tongue-in-cheek article, claims cyclists are at work on a "Stealth" mountain bike.

Mr. Coello also notes that today, one finds "mountain bikes . . . banned from trails in all national and most state parks and monuments, and they're partially or completely forbidden in an increasing number of city, county, and regional parks. They are allowed on the majority of national-forest (68,000 out of 100,000 miles) and Bureau of Land Management roads and trails, except those in wilderness and primitive areas and on a few specially marked trails."

On the one hand, hikers fear that cyclists will injure them and destroy the trails. On the other hand, cyclists feel they should have unlimited access to all public lands including wilderness areas. Cyclists, according to Coello, claim they "cause less trail damage than horses, which are ubiquitous in many backcountry areas." Cyclists feel they're in a "Catch-22" situation: motorists don't want cyclists on the road; hikers don't want them off the road.

The Sierra Club is the major group lobbying for hikers, and it was the Sierra Club that initially took a hard-core "no mountain bikes anywhere" stance. But, perhaps upon discovering that 17% of their own members rode mountain bikes, even the Sierra Club has softened . . . a little. For example, although "it no longer . . . lumps the bikes into the same category as . . . other terrain-marring off-road vehicles," it still officially opposes "the presence of mountain bikes on public lands and [together with] the California Department of Parks and Recreation is determined to close most state park trails to mountain bikers."

A fact pointed out by Alan Goldsmith, the owner of a large Santa Monica bike shop, is that "crowds and traffic forced bicyclists to escape from roads to off-roads and now the Santa Monica Mountains look like the Hollywood Freeway at rush hour."

Perhaps as a result of this, notes author Judy Pasternak, the "territory of bike riding in the Santa Monica Mountains [over the last year] has become more and more limited . . . [mountain bikes have been banned] from most trails in the area, allowing them for the most part only on wide, level fire roads built for emergency vehicles and dismissed by the bikers as unchallenging and less than scenic."

Doug Thomas of ROMP (Responsible Organized Mountain Pedalers) feels the responsibility for trail closures lies not with equestrians or hikers but with cyclists because we're "perceived as 16 year old kamikaze pilots who risk life and limb of all who get in our way."

ROMP president Jim Hunter stated in *Mountain Bike* magazine that "If we had enough political power it wouldn't matter when or how we rode or even if we tore hell out of the trails. We're going to be treated like a minority until we join the political process. Mountain bikers, however, are by nature an independent sort, tending to be apolitical rather than organizational."

But others have pointed out that "off-road cycling is introducing new areas to people who otherwise would never have gotten out there" says Dave Garoutte, founder of the Bicycle Trails Council of Marin County. "We're developing a whole new generation of environmentalists who want to keep open space undeveloped."

One solution has been for mountain bike clubs to cooperate with land managers. Mountain bicyclists now join with other groups in

cleaning up the mountains and building and rebuilding trails. In an article in "The California Bicyclist," Naomi Bloom notes that ". . . in the San Gabriel mountains the Mt. Wilson Bicycling Assn. is doing monthly volunteer trail work in the Angeles National Forest."

She also points out that ". . . in Pasadena, a group riding out of Alan Purnell's Pasadena Cyclery took on an improvement project on the popular Sunset Trail. To minimize erosion from skids, they dug out soft switchbacks, laid bricks and covered the bricks over. Then they laid railroad ties to act as 'passive restraints,' or speed bumps." In the Bay Area one group of cyclists instructs novice riders in the social graces of "trail etiquette."

Concerned Off-Road Bicyclists Assn. (CORBA) represents "the interests of mountain bikers in the Santa Monica Mountains in local policy-setting meetings." It and other local groups train volunteers to patrol the Santa Monicas and the San Gabriels.

As a result of these efforts, many rangers report that "they're getting more bikes than ever and having less trouble." Adds Karyn Kent of San Diego's Off-Road Bicycle Association, ". . . even the threat of environmental damage would have cancelled her club's race in January. Yet when the worst storm of the season settled over the course and produced wet, muddy trails, "they still felt we were not a threat to the environment."

I have ridden trails in the past, and I plan to ride more trails in the future. However, considering that mountain bikes may be banned from trails at almost any time, most of this book is devoted to routes for mountain bicycles on fireroads.

Some people also maintain that mountain bikers litter more than other recreation-area users and tell of finding paths desecrated with the fragments of shattered reflectors. After hearing of these "shattered reflectors," I decided to do my own survey. I made a note of every bicycle-created piece of trash that I saw. If I had the space I carried it out. In over 350 miles of riding to research this book, I found just five items which could have been left by cyclists. Five items too many—but among them, I found no reflectors.

"If there's a litter problem along the John Muir Trail, they don't exclude the backpackers from the trail," says Glenn Odell, former NORBA owner. "Those users are a given. But off-road bicycling is still suffering from a lack of clout, being the new kid on the block."

One of the changes that have taken place since the publication of *Mountain Bicycling in the San Gabriels* is the introduction of a new term, "single track." The first time I heard this term, I was at Mount

Waterman. In the summer months, Mount Waterman allows cyclists and their bikes to ride up the chair lifts and to ride their bikes down. When I asked other cyclists for the best way down, they said it was "the single track."

Now, since Waterman is a ski resort, were they referring to a ski route, since in skiing you follow tracks, or were they referring to the tracks left by one of the caterpillar tractors? In any event, I couldn't figure out how either a skier or a tractor could leave only one track. But instead I learned that it refers to a trail so narrow that cyclists can ride only one abreast, and hence leave only a "single track."

Equipment

I used a bicycle in the $400 range (1985 price) to research the trips for this book. After I went to wider rims and changed its stock 1.75-inch combination street/off-road tires to 2-inch knobby tires, it was completely satisfactory.

Today, manufacturers even produce different tread patterns for the front and rear wheels. The rear tires I'm currently using have a very aggressive tread for maximum traction, while the fronts have a less aggressive tread in the center but have more tread extending out to the sides, for better cornering.

I have had very few punctures—only 3 in the past 5 years. I attribute this partly to luck and partly to the fact that I use Mr. Tuffy, a vinyl boot, which is inserted between the tire and the tube.

Even though I've had few punctures, I've had quite a few defective valves recently. Because of this, I now carry an extra valve and use the metal valve caps (found in automotive-supply stores), which have a rubber seal and double as a tool to remove the valve.

Although my bike came equipped with a quick-release seatpost, to allow the seat to be lowered when descending, it soon became tiring and impractical to stop and readjust the seatpost every time I began to ascend. A clever solution to this problem is Breeze and Angell's Hite-Rite, a spring that attaches to the seatpost and to the seatpost clamp. When descending you release the clamp and allow your body's weight to push the seat down. When climbing, you release the clamp and the spring pops the seat back to its normal position. I'm long-legged, and I found that their longer Xtra-Hite model was perfect for me.

Another clever device is Tailwind's Shoulder Holder. Distributed by Specialized, it combines a shoulder strap, for carrying the bike over obstacles, with a small bag (just enough room for a tube, a patch kit, and a small crescent wrench).

On a bike that sometimes may be ridden for miles with the rear brakes applied, excellent brakes are a necessity. Most riders agree that premium-quality brake pads, such as the Mathauser, are well worth their extra cost.

I've been searching for almost 15 years for the perfect chain lubricant. Mountain bicycling makes the chain lubricant's job even more difficult by adding dirt and water to the elements to which the chain is exposed. I keep alternating between a "clean" teflon lubricant and one of the many oil lubes.

TOE CLIPS: When mountain bikes first arrived toe clips were generally not used, the general feeling being that in case of a fall you would want to get your foot out as quickly as possible. However, I find that toe clips give the same advantage as on the road—the ability to increase your pedaling efficiency. I use the wider, nylon toe clip, which companies such as Specialized introduced especially for mountain bikes. I just leave the toe straps fairly loose or flip the pedals over.

GEARING: For years there have been nonround chainwheels on the market. But a few years ago the Bio-Pace chainwheel was introduced, a nonround shape developed with the help of a computer to allow more efficient pedaling. It is supposed to help climbing. I use one, but can't tell any difference in climbing (I'm still slow). However, for me Bio-Pace makes shifting onto the small chainring much easier.

Hazards and Dangers

In one respect, I think off-road riding is less hazardous than riding on the road: you are much less exposed to motor vehicles. However, you will probably fall more while riding on dirt, and each time you fall, you risk injury.

In over 40,000 miles of road cycling, I've had about half a dozen spills, none serious. I probably fell at least that many times in my first six months of owning a mountain bike. Of course, it has to be safer to fall onto dirt at 10 mph than to fall onto asphalt at 40 mph.

BRAKES: When riding on pavement, the rear brakes don't have to be used much. The fronts do the stopping, the rears keep the back wheel from skidding in a panic stop. I had gotten in the habit of almost never using my rear brakes. It took time to change this habit, because on dirt, just the opposite is true. The rear brakes do most of the stopping, and aggressive application of the front brakes could initiate the "head plant," a highly unpopular skiing maneuver.

HELMETS: I strongly recommend wearing a good hard helmet. Unfortunately, many cyclists who would never think of diving head first into the ground think nothing of subjecting themselves to the same risk by riding without a helmet.

Several makers have responded to the market with helmets especially designed for the mountain bike. But in a search for lighter and lighter helmets, the current trend is to the soft-shell helmet. This is a helmet with the shock-absorbing foam of the hard helmet but without its hard outer shell. It has at least two problems. First, mountain bicycling has an additional hazard, usually not found on paved roads: rocks. If you were unlucky enough to land on a sharp rock, it could, in theory, pierce the foam of a soft helmet. Second, it's a fairly fragile helmet. I store my family's bicycles upside down in our garage, and I hang our helmets from the handlebars. The rest of the family has trouble even reaching the bikes or the helmets. But I'm tall, and about once a month I knock a helmet off a bike and onto the ground. Such abuse would finish a soft-shell helmet.

I'll stick to hard helmets, on and off the road.

I wish I could say that I always wear my helmet. I have seen research that shows that in hot weather body temperature is no higher for the helmeted rider. But my forehead hasn't seen this report and it doesn't just sweat, it *leaks*. So much perspiration runs down my face that I'm unable to see. As a result, in hot weather, I wear a sweat band, and strap my helmet to the bike when climbing.

GLOVES: The bicycle glove is another safety item. Today bicycle gloves are seen everywhere. They're popular with weight-lifters and break dancers, and like cycling shorts they've become fashionable streetwear. But their main purpose, in case of a fall, is to protect your hands from cuts and abrasions. On a road bike they can be used to wipe the tires after riding through debris. On a mountain bike they can also be used to absorb road shock, especially if the glove is padded. My wife likes a glove, heavily padded with Spenco, but I find that too much padding detracts from the feeling of control.

RATTLESNAKES: One hazard that exists in the local mountains is the rattlesnake. Still, although I saw many deer, quail, other kinds of snakes, lizards, etc., in over 350 miles of riding to research this book, I saw no rattlesnake. However, I did discover that a twig, caught in the rear triangle or derailleur and hitting the spokes can make a good enough imitation of the rattler's sound to make my hair stand on end.

POISON OAK: Another, much more common hazard is poison oak. It's found only on lower-elevation rides. Mugwort, a silver-leaved companion plant to poison oak, generally grows nearby. I can spot mugwort more readily than poison oak, and usually see it first. I have found that if I rub my skin with the mugwort leaf, the oil from the poison oak is neutralized. It works for me, but I know others who say it doesn't work for them.

FLUID REPLACEMENT: Most of the rides in this book have very limited or no sources of drinking water. In warm weather, I carry at least two water bottles and before the ride I drink, drink, drink.

A new product on the market in the past few years is electrolytic replacement fluid. These are claimed to do what the name says—replace electrolytes lost through sweat. I first discovered them on a double century. I was having a bad day and at about 140 miles I had "hit the wall." Another rider offered me some of his "magic potion." At the next hill, I sprinted, and the rest of the ride was a cinch. I was intrigued.

Then I climbed Mt. Whitney as a day hike. I expected my wife to leave me in her dust, because usually she is the stronger hiker. She ate all day and drank water. Except for maybe a half a muffin for breakfast, all I had was a swallow of the electrolyte replacement fluid every 10 minutes. After about 2 hours it was as if an afterburner had cut in. I had incredible energy all day. My lovely and usually inexhaustible wife was worn out. I was convinced.

A trick for hot-weather riding is to insert your water bottle into a sock. Keep the sock wet, and the evaporation keeps the water amazingly cool.

RIDING ALONE: Although I know riding alone is potentially dangerous, one great advantage of bicycling as a sport is that you don't need a partner, Still, a major fear of mine is to have an accident and be immobilized in a remote area. Therefore, I leave my intended route either on an answering machine, on a note left with my family, or on the windshield of my car. In case the worst should happen, I carry extra food, water, and a mylar survival blanket in my bike bag.

INSECTS: Except for the possibility, which now exists even in Southern California, of contracting Lyme disease through a tick bite, the numerous insects found in the mountains are more annoying than hazardous. I consider insect repellent an absolute must. I once forgot to bring it along on a 35-mile ride. Whenever I stopped, I would be attacked, so except for one spot where it is usually windy enough to blow them away, I had to keep moving. The insects turned a normally enjoyable ride into a miserable ordeal.

As for Lyme disease, cyclists ride high and avoid riding directly through brush, so perhaps they will be safe from the ticks that carry it.

SUNSCREEN: These days, with the protection of the ozone layer gradually diminishing, the use of sunscreen is increasingly recommended. You can still have a tan. Just use sunscreen to prevent excessive aging and possible skin cancer. However, remember that anything over SPF #15 is likely to irritate the skin.

TOILET PAPER: I carry some rolled-up toilet paper in a plastic bag just in case.

EMERGENCIES: While researching this book, I met my exact opposite. He was about ready to head up into a canyon and asked to borrow my pump. He had no pump, no apparent patch kit or spare tube. He wore cycling shorts, but no gloves, helmet, or even shoes— he wore sandals.

The new mountain cyclist may still have the "road-racing mindset" of never carrying an extra ounce on the bike. Any emergency can be handled by plastic money, hitching a ride, phoning home, or phoning 911. On the road, if you "hit the wall," food and fluids are as close as the nearest liquor store. But in the wilderness the credit card is worthless, and few cars, fewer phones, and no liquor stores exist.

TOOLS: The number of tools I carry depends on the length of the trip. For short rides of up to 4 or 5 miles from my car, home or major road, I carry a pump, a patch kit, a spare tube, and a small crescent wrench in the Shoulder Holder. If something breaks, I can walk out.

On longer trips, where I might be 15 miles from a road, I carry the above plus a second spare tube, a chain tool, allen wrenches, a screwdriver, and spare rear-brake and derailleur cables.

Mountain Bicycling Regulations

The National Off-Road Bicycling Association (NORBA) has put together 10 rules of conduct to promote mountain bicycling safety, to educate the cyclist in minimal environmental impact, and to help counter anti-cycling propaganda.

"Off-pavement bicycling can open exciting new horizons for you. In order to maximize the benefit of your adventure and maintain the quality of the experience for those who will follow you, we urge you to adopt this code as your own.

1. I will yield the right of way to other nonmotorized recreationists. I realize that people judge all cyclists by my actions.

2. I will slow down and use caution when approaching or overtaking another and will make my presence known well in advance.

3. I will maintain control of my speed at all times and will approach turns in anticipation of someone around the bend.

4. I will stay on designated trails to avoid trampling native vegetation and will minimize potential erosion to trails by not using muddy trails or short-cutting switchbacks.

5. I will not disturb wildlife or livestock.

6. I will not litter. I will pack out what I pack in and pack out more than my share whenever possible.

7. I will respect public and private property, including trail use signs, and no trespassing signs, and I will leave gates as I have found them.

8. I will always be self-sufficient and my destination objective and travel speed will be determined by my ability, my equipment, the terrain, [and] the present and potential weather conditions.

9. I will not travel solo when bikepacking in a remote area. I will leave word of my destination and when I plan to return.

10. I will observe the practice of minimum-impact bikepacking by, 'taking only pictures and memories, and leaving only waffle prints.'

Trip Classifications

Trip distances: I measured the distances for the trips with a Cat-Eye 1000 Cyclometer.

Time: Time includes average rest stops, lunch stops, calls of nature, and general exploring. I consider myself an average cyclist in terms of speed.

Elevation gain: Elevation gains were calculated from topographic maps. The figures are for total gain, not net.

Difficulty: Trips are classified for difficulty according to time and elevation gain. Easy trips take 1–2 hours and involve little climbing. Moderate trips take 3–4 hours and climb 1 to 2000 feet. Strenuous trips take 5 to 8 hours and may climb 3 to 4000 feet.

Topo: This refers to the 7½ minute topographic maps that cover each trip. These can be purchased at many local backpacking shops and map stores, or (without paying sales tax) at the Federal Building, Room 7638, 300 N. Los Angeles Street, Los Angeles.

Thomas Bros: The start can be located on the indicated map and section of the *Los Angeles County, Orange County, San Bernardino County,* or *Ventura County Thomas Brothers' Map Book.* If the county is not stated, it is Los Angeles.

Other family activities: Although I see more and more families mountain-bicycling together, they are still the exception. So I have included some other activities that the noncycling members of a family can enjoy while the cyclists are riding.

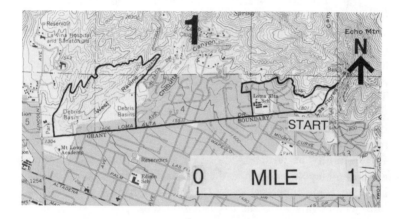

The Trips

Trip 1

Altadena Crest One

Distance: 6.09 miles
Time: 1½ hours
Elevation gain: 500 feet
Difficulty: Moderate
Topo: Pasadena
Thomas Bros map: page 20, section B3

When the Spanish ruled California, they could apparently see the flowering foothills of what is today Altadena from San Pedro Harbor (not impossible, since on a clear day you can easily see San Pedro Harbor from Altadena). This ride starts at an elevation of 1800 feet, at the corner of Lake Avenue and Loma Alta Drive near the mouth of Las Flores (Spanish for "the flowers") Canyon.

You enter to the right of the old wrought-iron gate and begin riding on the dirt foot trail. As soon as possible, leave the dirt and ride onto the paved road to your left. This was the driveway of the old Cobb Estate. This 107-acre estate has been attracting people's attention and inflaming their curiosity for more than 60 years. It was originally settled by a Robert Forsyth. Then, in 1893, a miner, William Twaddel, used gold recovered from Las Flores Canyon to purchase the property.

Charles H. Cobb was born in Maine and worked as a logger when he was just 16. In 1876 he went to Seattle, where he made a fortune in the lumber industry. When Cobb bought the acreage, in 1917, Twaddel still lived on the property in a home built by Forsyth.

Cobb's wife ran the estate, which included an orange grove. Cobb had an office in Pasadena, and his adopted son had his father set him up in the automobile-repair business. Although the business failed, the building, with its sealed-off, arched vehicle entryways, still stands at the corner of Lake and Marcheta Avenue in Altadena, just below Webster's Pharmacy.

When Cobb, an enthusiastic Mason, died in 1939 at the age of 87, the home was transformed into a Masonic residence. Then, from 1942 until 1955, it served as a retreat for the nuns of St. Luke's Hospital. It was then purchased by a construction company, which unsuccessfully tried to develop the property. The home was vandalized, then demolished, and in 1960 Groucho, Harpo, and Gummo Marx bought the property, in a failed attempt to turn it into a cemetery. The property was then sold at auction, and was turned over by the buyer to the Forest Service to be managed as a wildlife refuge.

You may see some numbered signs. In the 1960s a pamphlet was prepared describing the many unique plants of the area. Copies of the pamphlet can still be obtained from the Altadena Library, but in the more than 20 years since the signs were put up, many have been destroyed, some of the described plants have died and disappeared, and plants differing from the descriptions have taken their place.

At mile 0.10 the road curves to the left, and at mile 0.28 you come to a Y. You can take either branch to ride around the foundation of the old Cobb house. Then the pavement steepens and becomes slippery, because of gravel, and then turns into a dirt road, used for access to water reservoirs farther up the canyon.

At mile 0.40, after 10 minutes of climbing, you come to a drinking fountain, constructed from rock. Here on the western edge of Las Flores Canyon you can see the beginnings of the Sam Merrill Trail as it snakes its way up the east side of the canyon to Echo Mountain.

After a drink, you turn around and start to ride downhill, but immediately turn right (west) up the first, extremely steep trail. From this trail, below you and to your left, you can see what was once a very elaborately constructed reservoir for the Cobb Estate.

At mile 0.72, you arrive at a spot that on a clear day gives an excellent view from Echo Mountain to Whittier's Rose Hills, Santiago Peak, San Pedro Harbor, Catalina Island, Palos Verdes, Santa Monica Bay, the San Rafael Hills, the Santa Monicas, the Verdugos and Mt. Lukens. Right in front of you is Lake Avenue, looking from here like a slightly bent arrow.

Almost every local newspaper article on mountain bikes mentions conflicts between equestrians and cyclists. In reality, you seldom run into horses. This trail is an exception. Because Altadena is still zoned for horses, many residents have horses and many nonresidents board their horses in the foothills. So this trail is extremely popular with the horse set. Be extra courteous.

An 1876-foot summit is reached at mile 0.91, and then at mile 0.97 you come to unsigned Monterosa Drive. You cross it and continue riding on the trail. You may see witches' hair, an orange parasitic plant beside the trail. It looks dry, but if you stop and inspect some, you'll discover that it is really rather moist.

This part of the trail is extremely eroded, but to make up for that you are near some very rural property with farm animals. At 1.29 miles you cross unsigned Canon Boulevard and enter a section that always has several dogs. Thank God for chain-link fences. You'll notice that there is beginning to be as much horse manure as dirt, and then at 1.41 miles you'll come to some horse property with corrals. Here you turn left onto unsigned but paved Skylane Drive.

At the end of this road, you turn left onto unmarked Vinehill Drive, and then at the end of the block you turn right onto Canon (still unsigned). At 1.72 miles you turn right onto Loma Alta. If you're tired, you can turn left and be back at the start in ¼ mile. Otherwise continue downhill. Here you can really let the bike go, because the next turn is not until the flashing yellow light, which you can see about ¼ mile ahead.

At 2.55 miles, after descending to 1460 feet, you turn right onto the Chaney Trail. This is one of the steepest paved roads in the area, and your reduced speed will allow you to notice that you're riding by a nursery (nurseries were one of the original "main industries" of Altadena). You come to a wide spot in the road and a gate (usually open) at the intersection of Alzada Drive. Here, the Forest Service turns back motorists on weekends when the capacity of parking at the top of the Chaney Trail and at Millard Campground has been exceeded. Being on a bicycle, you can pedal right past any roadblock. After 3.04 miles and 46 minutes you come to some white dots in the road. Here you turn left onto a trail. At 3.20 miles you veer left and begin a heavily eroded descent. After almost ½ mile of descending, you climb, descend, and then climb back to 1600 feet again, until you can see Loma Alta Park. At 4.29 miles the trail turns left and you parallel the park. At 4.39 miles after 1 hour of riding you turn left onto Loma Alta.

At the intersection of Lake and Loma Alta you come to the gates of the old Cobb Estate once more, and after 6.09 miles and 1½ hours the end of the ride.

Trip 2

Altadena Crest Two

Distance: 6.27 miles
Time: 1¼ hours
Elevation gain: 750 feet
Difficulty: Moderate to difficult
Topo: Pasadena, Mount Wilson
Thomas Bros map: page 20, section B3

This ride starts at 1800 feet, at the corner of Lake Avenue and Loma Alta Drive in Altadena. You enter to the right of the Cobb Estate's old wrought-iron gate and ride on the dirt foot trail until, at the end of the fence at mile 0.12, you go left and descend into Las Flores Canyon. Do not take the upper trail, which goes to Echo Mountain and has been recently posted NO BIKES.

At the junction at the bottom of Las Flores Canyon, you turn right, and at mile 0.27 you cross an unsigned paved road and continue riding on the trail. You catch a glimpse of the San Gabriel Valley and then the trail actually crosses over a front yard. You follow the trail as it parallels a fence to the left. At mile 0.45, at the end of the fence, you turn left onto an asphalt road. Immediately you go right, cross the flood-control channel and turn left onto a wide dirt trail that parallels the flood-control channel. As you make your way downstream, you encounter a very steep descent just before turning left onto paved but unsigned Rubio Canyon Road.

At 1.04 miles, after a 22-minute descent to 1600 feet, just after the DIP sign, you turn left onto Zane Grey Terrace. Zane Grey, the famous author of Western tales, had two houses in Altadena, and one of them used to be on this road. At 2857 Zane Grey you turn left onto the driveway and then merge onto the signed Altadena Crest Trail.

At 1.49 miles, after 10 minutes of hard climbing, you come to some asphalt. Ride down the asphalt, turn left and begin riding on the dirt trail once more.

At 2.51 miles, after 38 minutes, you reach a 1720-foot summit from which you can view Santiago Peak, Rose Hills, the harbor of San Pedro, Catalina Island, Palos Verdes, Baldwin Hills, Santa Monica Bay, the Santa Monica Mountains, and the Verdugo Hills.

Now you make a steep descent, until you make a right turn onto the paved, unsigned Mount Wilson Toll Road at 3.41 miles. On it you make a steep climb, pass through a gate in a chain-link fence, and turn right onto unsigned Pinecrest Drive. Stay on Pinecrest, then make a right turn onto Altadena Drive. At the signal at Lake Avenue you turn right and begin the climb back to the Cobb Estate, which is reached at 6.27 miles after 1¼ hours.

NOTE: This ride can be combined with Altadena Crest One to make a ride of 12½ miles and 2¾ hours.

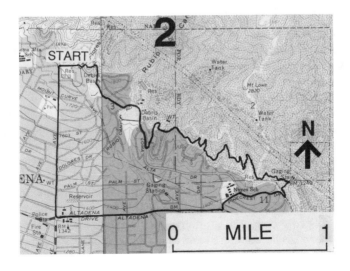

Trip 3

San Rafael Romp

Distance: 11.61 miles
Time: 1¾ hours
Elevation gain: 1000 feet
Difficulty: Moderate
Topo: Pasadena
Thomas Bros map: page 26, section E4

At the time of writing, the City of Glendale had closed Scholl Canyon because of a methane leak. It is expected to reopen in the spring of 1990. Before attempting this ride, call 818-956-2000 to see if it has been reopened.

In 1784 Jose Maria Verdugo acquired grazing rights to most of the land west of the Arroyo Seco from the governor of Alta California and named it Rancho San Rafael. It was only the second rancho in California. It was wild enough land that in those days visitors to the Verdugo property were escorted by armed vaqueros who used their guns to scare away grizzly bears.

Later it was purchased by Robert Alexander Campbell-Johnston. He built a replica of a Scottish country church, which was used in the movie "Going My Way" and still exists on Avenue 64. And he named this area Annandale after his ancestral home in Dumphries Shire, Scotland.

The area was still so rural that in the 1920's the Annandale Country Club's cook would catch 25–30 trout from the nearby Arroyo Seco a couple of mornings each week to serve at breakfast and lunches. And there are records of two gold mines being dug on the golf-course property.

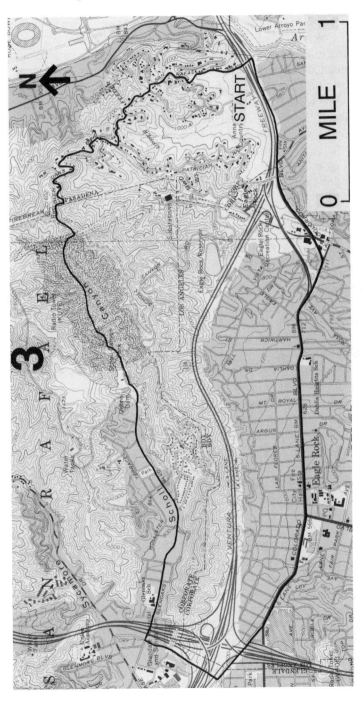

This ride starts at 800 feet, near the corner of San Rafael Blvd. and Colorado Blvd. You can park your car on San Rafael, just north of the 134 Freeway and just across the street from the entrance to the Annandale Country Club.

At 0.26 miles you ride past 220 San Rafael Blvd. This former private residence is the Kresge Seismological Lab, operated by Caltech. When you hear of an earthquake being "measured" by Caltech, this is where it's measured.

After 10 minutes of climbing to 1120 feet, at mile 0.61 you turn left onto Glen Oaks Blvd. You have a short downhill, but soon begin climbing again. You keep following Glen Oaks even when it says NO OUTLET. It's surprising that even in this area of extremely high fire hazard, many roofs are wooden. And notice the "Wagon Wheel" window in the house opposite Fairlawn Drive.

Now you begin to see the views that make this area popular, and after 32 minutes you come to a gate at 2.17 miles and carry your bike over it. The road turns to dirt and you pass several spare off-road tires. At 2.43 miles, about 50 yards before a chain-link fence, you make a sharp right turn and begin climbing. At 2.55 miles bear left and begin a slight downhill.

In 1906 the *Glendale News* said "one may lose oneself in . . . Scholl's Canyon, silent and untouched by civilization." However, today, Scholl Canyon (now on your left) is the source of the slightly unpleasant odor you may now be detecting, because it has been used as a landfill since 1963.

Then, at 2.82 miles, you begin to climb, and through a notch to your right, you can see Pasadena and the San Gabriel range for the first time. At 3.17 miles, after 49 minutes, almost all of it climbing, you arrive at a 1480-foot summit. You have a choice of 3 roads. Take the middle road, which curves to the right and descends.

You pass some beehives and then, at 3.60 miles, after 55 minutes of riding, you reach pavement once more. At 3.95 and at 4.25 miles you have to walk your bike around locked gates and at 5.39 miles you come to the intersection with Glenoaks Canyon Road and continue riding on Glenoaks Blvd.

At 6.90 miles you take a left onto Harvey Drive. After riding underneath the freeway, turn left onto Broadway, which swings to the left, descends to 600 feet, and merges with Colorado Blvd.

At 10.15 miles you continue on Colorado by bearing left. At the light at 11.51 miles you turn left onto San Rafael. Finally, you return to the starting point at 11.61 miles after 1¾ hours.

Church of the Angels on Avenue 64

Trip 4

Flint Peak

Distance: 1.50 miles
Time: 45 minutes
Elevation gain: 400 feet
Difficulty: Moderate to difficult
Topo: Pasadena
Thomas Bros map: page 19, section C2

Frank Flint was born in Massachusetts in 1862, but he was raised and educated in San Francisco. He started a law practice in Los Angeles, became a judge, then a U.S. attorney, and in 1904 became a United States senator for one term. He helped bring Owens County water to Los Angeles and so could be viewed as a good guy or a bad guy, depending upon the times and your viewpoint.

At the turn of the century he began purchasing land in the Glendale and La Canada areas, including a good-sized portion of what had been Rancho San Rafael. Senator Flint, an equestrian, designed a community of large, luxurious homes on large estates connected with a system of over 20 miles of still-existing horseriding trails (from which mountain bikes are today completely prohibited). He wanted the area, though close to Los Angeles, to give its residents the illusion of living in the country. He named it after himself: Flintridge.

He lost a large amount of money in the 1929 stock-market crash and died while on a cruise ship in the Philippines.

This ride starts at the 1560-foot end of Figueroa Blvd., just beyond the intersection of Marengo. This area has changed rapidly.

About three years ago my daughter had an appointment in the area, and instead of waiting in the car for her, I rode my bike to Flint Peak. Then, the area had no homes. Today some are already on the used housing market.

You carry your bike over the metal gate and begin a short but steep and sandy climb. At the top of this slope, you are rewarded by a view of the San Gabriels, Pasadena, Brookside Park, the Rose Bowl (wouldn't this be a great spot to view the Rose Bowl's fireworks?), and just below you, Pasadena's Art Center School.

You continue climbing up the hill to your right. This is extremely steep and slippery, too steep and slippery for me to ride the bike, and almost too slippery to push the bike. From the top of this hill you get an even better view of Pasadena, and on a weekday, you can hear the earth-moving equipment at the nearby Scholl Canyon landfill.

At mile 0.30 the road becomes paved for a short way, then you continue climbing until at mile 0.75, after 20 minutes, you reach a usually locked gate and the 1889-foot summit of Flint Peak. From here you can see Griffith Park, the Verdugos, Cerro Negro, the San Gabriels and Pasadena.

Here you can contemplate the future of Southern California. Almost all of the nearby hills have been developed, and each house must be supplied with water, gas, power, sewer, and trash pickup. And in back of us is the current local solution to the trash problem: a canyon being filled with it.

Across the canyon to the north you can see a water tower and some older, red-tile-roofed buildings. This was the Flintridge Biltmore Hotel. It featured magnificent views of the Arroyo Seco, the San Gabriels (then called the Sierra Madres), and the Pacific Ocean. Senator Flint finished it in 1928, but soon the Depression was in full swing. Since it had $30 rooms, and was very isolated and difficult to reach, it was losing money, and it was sold to the Catholic Diocese. Since then it has been operated as the Sacred Heart Academy, a Catholic girl's high school.

On your way back down, all roads begin to look alike. At 1.23 miles, at a fire hydrant, take the middle paved road, which goes uphill. At the top of this hill take the road to the right. Then, at 1.44 miles, you go left. This hill isn't any less steep going down, so lower your saddle and attempt the descent, or dismount and walk down. At 1.48 miles you go left at the bottom of the hill, to return to the start at 1.56 miles after 45 minutes.

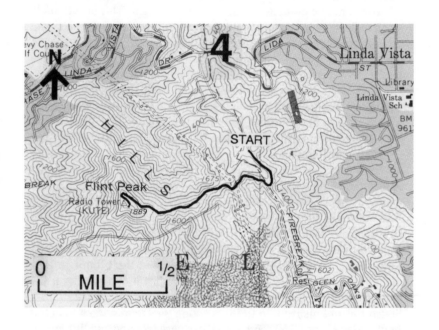

Trip 5

Flintridge Figure Eight

Distance: 9.45 miles
Time: 2¾ hours
Elevation gain: 1300 feet
Difficulty: Moderate
Topo: Pasadena
Thomas Bros map: page 19, section B3

This ride starts from 1300-foot Descanso Gardens. You can park in the lot or on the street. Descanso has water, restrooms, and a snack bar. You go southeast on Descanso Drive, until at mile 0.35 you turn right onto the Padres Trail and then immediately turn left onto Forest Hill Drive. This is a fairly hard even though paved climb, but you are rewarded with some great views. At mile 0.78, no house has yet been built and you get a panoramic view of almost the entire San Gabriel range.

At mile 0.86, after about 12 minutes of riding, you come to a locked gate that marks the start of the dirt portion. The more skilled rider probably does not have to dismount, but I had to get off and walk my bike between the exposed granite cliff and the left side of the gate.

At 1.18 miles you take a side trip by turning left onto a trail. At 1.37 miles you reach a lookout point with the foundation of an old tower, from which you can see both the Verdugos and the entire San Gabriel range.

At 1.78 miles, after returning to the main road, you come to a concrete water tower. Here you turn left onto another road, which passes some beehives under the powerlines.

At 1.93 miles, after 49 minutes of climbing, to 1680 feet, you come to another junction, where you turn left and begin descending.

Five minutes bring you to a gate at 2.61 miles. Here we begin riding on pavement again. You pass the entrance to the Cherry Canyon Nature Trail (which, if you've ever visited it, you know might be renamed a National Poison Oak Refuge). This nature trail was acquired by the Santa Monica Mountain Nature Conservancy in 1985. At 2.68 miles you turn right onto Hampstead Road, and 3.32 miles, just after passing Stratford Drive, you pass a streambed.

You keep descending on Hampstead to 1400 feet, until at 3.80 miles, with Flint Peak straight ahead, you turn right onto Sugar Loaf Drive. This is a very steep climb which, even in my lowest gear, forced me to tack the bike back and forth.

You walk the bike around another locked gate and leave the pavement. At 4.44 miles, after 1:26, you reach a plateau that offers a good view. For an even better view, ride up to the area surrounding the old 1887-foot fire lookout tower on Cerro Negro. From here you get a 360° view. On a clear day you can see Santiago Peak, San Pedro Harbor, Catalina Island, Palos Verdes, Santa Monica Bay, the Channel Islands, Griffith Park, the Santa Monicas, and the entire San Gabriel range. Right in front of you are the Verdugos.

At 5.12 miles, after 1:40, you turn left, through the gate, onto the asphalt road. The elaborate wall-lined road to the right of this leads to a police training facility where the POLICE DOGS OFF LEASH and LIVE AMMUNITION signs certainly kept me from further exploration.

From here you descend on the wide, badly deteriorated asphalt road. At 5.94 miles the road becomes smoothly paved and levels off. At 6.01 miles you turn right onto Fern (unsigned) and at 6.18 miles you reach a gate that may be locked but is passable. In ½ mile you reach Verdugo Road and turn right. At 7.15 miles you reach Oakwood Avenue, where there is a market. At 8.38 miles you turn right onto Verdugo Blvd. Here there are many liquor stores and fast-food restaurants. At 9.19 miles you turn right onto Descanso, and soon reach the start at 9.45 miles after 2¾ hours.

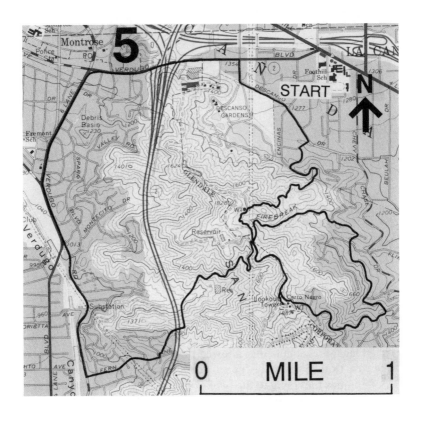

Trip 6

Debs Regional Park

Distance: 2.99 miles
Time: 1 hour
Elevation gain: 400 feet
Difficulty: Easy, with one steep hill and one moderate hill
Topo: Los Angeles
Thomas Bros map: Page 36, section C3
Other Family Activities: Note: although this is a regional park with grassy fields and picnic areas, the amount of graffiti indicates heavy gang activity.

The area surrounding the Arroyo Seco, south of the Devil's Gate dam, has had a colorful history. Just before the turn of the century, an elevated wooden bikeway was built to connect Pasadena's Green Hotel with Los Angeles. The bikeway was such a failure that the only surviving picture shows a car, not a bike, using it. But it established legal precedents that allowed the Pasadena Freeway, the first freeway, to take virtually the same route to Los Angeles. And the communities that cling to the banks of the Arroyo still contain many buildings that represent the back-to-nature style of the Craftsmen era of the 1910s and 1920s.

John Philip Sousa stayed in the home that bears his name when he visited the music professor of Occidental College. Singer Jackson Browne's father built the churchlike Abbey House. And the men who built the tiles and stained windows for the Greene and Greene houses of Pasadena lived and worked near the Arroyo.

Therefore, knowing the artsy, liberal history of the community, you could make the assumption that Debs Park is named for

Socialist labor leader and Presidential candidate Eugene V. Debs. You would be wrong. It is named for former Los Angeles County Supervisor Ernest E. Debs.

Leased from the City of Los Angeles in 1967, Ernest E. Debs Regional Park is off of Monterey Road in the Montecito Heights section of the city of Los Angeles. From the Pasadena Freeway take the Via Marisol exit and drive southeast 0.30 mile to Monterey Road. Turn right on Monterey and after 0.70 mile, beyond a cut in the hills, turn right into the park. After slowly crossing over the 12 speed bumps that slow the traffic, you reach the parking lot after another 0.7 mile.

From the 620-foot parking lot, you take the gated, asphalt road that leaves from the north (not the ungated, concrete path from the west). This immediately becomes a very steep climb requiring a shift into the lowest gear. Then at mile 0.29 it mercifully levels off. At mile 0.33, with a small man-made lake to your left, you climb the paved footpath to the top of a grassy knoll.

From the top of this 800-foot knoll, on a clear winter's day, you can see the San Gabriels, snow-capped Mount Baldy and San Gorgonio Mountain, Orange County's Santiago Peak, the nearby Monterey Hills, the Sears building rising like a chrome monolith, Long Beach Harbor, Catalina Island, and Palos Verdes. Some trees on the western edge of the knoll block what would be a complete 360° view.

After absorbing the view you descend on a paved path toward the lake. At the junction with the main road at mile 0.39, turn right. Then at the junction at mile 0.43 the main road swings to the left.

You pass a closed restroom, make another climb, level off, and then descend, passing a huge, graffiti-covered shelter.

At mile 0.79, just before reaching a turnaround that is the end of the road, you come to an 840-foot junction with two dirt roads. Take the one to the right. At mile 0.85 you arrive at a junction beside four telephone poles lying on the ground. Leave the main road and take the path to the right, which takes you out onto a ridge. At the end of this ridge, at mile 0.89, you make an extremely steep descent onto a single track marked by an oak tree with a blue arrow. At mile 0.85 you are forced to ride over or around a fallen log. Then you pass an interesting old deteriorated concrete structure which, with its many tight openings, reminds me of the home of some make-believe creature. At 0.96 miles, at the yellow, wooden post, go left. At 1.01 miles you come to an upside-down 1959 Impala, in which someone must have had an interesting ride. At this point the trail becomes a road

once more. Go left at the junction at 1.24 miles, right at the junction
at 1.43 miles, and left at the 4-way junction at 1.74 miles. Although
this became an official regional park recently, it has served as a park
for 40 or 50 years and has many cement steps and other structures
dating from earlier times.

At the junction at 1.87 miles you take the road that goes up and
to the right. Then at the curve at 1.99 miles notice the cathedral-like
structure on the other side of the freeway. This is the Southwest
Museum, started by anthropologist Charles Lummis and today considered one of the finest American Indian museums anywhere. The
asphalt ramp below you is a Soap Box Derby track dating from the
1950's.

At 2.51 miles, after 45 minutes, you are back at the paved road.
Turn right onto it and at 2.68 miles come to the man-made lake. You
follow the dirt path just above the left shoreline. From the lake, you
can see downtown Los Angeles, a skyline that is no longer dominated by City Hall, Santa Monica Bay, Dodger Stadium, the Southwest Museum again, parts of Griffith Park, including Mt. Lee, and
even the San Gabriel range's Mt. Lukens.

At 2.73 miles, by the pine tree with the blue graffiti, you go left
onto the road, which descends along a ridge. At 2.91 miles you turn
left onto a cement path, reaching the parking lot at 2.99 miles after a
little over one hour of riding.

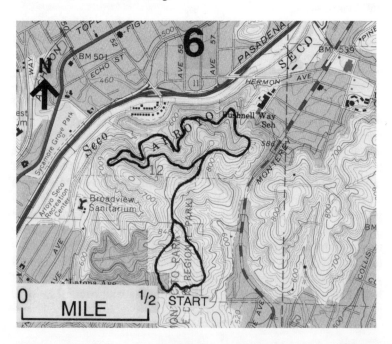

Trip 7

Brand

Distance: 6.43 miles
Time: 2¾ hours
Elevation gain: 2000 feet
Difficulty: Strenuous
Topo: Burbank, Pasadena
Thomas Bros map: page 18, section B6
Other family activities: Playground, library, art gallery, nature trail, Japanese gardens, doctors' house.

Glendale has a Brand Boulevard, a Brand Park, a Brand Library, a Brand school, and many "Brand" businesses. Why, then, is Leslie Brand's life virtually unknown in Glendale?

Brand was born near St. Louis to a wealthy family, and entered the real-estate and title-insurance business in that area. After his first wife died, he moved to Los Angeles and established a new title-insurance business. Thinking it would be a good investment, he began buying land in the Glendale area.

Many cities' main thoroughfares are named Main Street or Central Avenue. Yet Glendale's Brand Boulevard, not Central Avenue, is its center of business. That is because after Central Avenue was its main street, Brand began buying up property several blocks to the west, renamed a minor street Brand Boulevard, and along with Henry Huntington, used it as a streetcar right-of-way, to connect Glendale with Los Angeles.

This caused the value of the property along what should have been Glendale's main business street to plummet and left a bad taste for Mister Brand in the mouths of many of Glendale's citizens.

This ride starts from Glendale's 800-foot Brand Park, which used to be the private estate of Brand. When he died in 1925, his will directed that his wife be allowed to remain in their house but that upon her death the house and surrounding 488 acres were to be turned over to the city of Glendale. It was stipulated that the property would remain Glendale's only as long as it was called Brand Park and only as long as his former residence was called the Brand Library.

When he was alive, Brand wanted the house to be known as El Miradero (Spanish for "the lookout"), but locals preferred to call it Brand's Castle. It is a combination of Taj Mahal exterior and a Victorian interior. These days it serves as both a branch library in the Glendale system and an art gallery. The nearby Japanese Garden and Tea House honors Glendale's sister city of Higashiosaka.

From the parking lot next to the library, you ride around the gate and head up the paved road that leads past a restored Victorian house. Built in 1888 and used by a series of doctors as an office/residence, today it is known as the "doctor's house". At mile 0.07 you come to a gate that is difficult to get around. I pushed the bike through the horizontal bars of the gate.

At mile 0.15 you take the farthest paved road to the right. The oasis-like setting and the old foundation are all that remain of the private country club that Brand built above his main house in 1909 for $10,000. It featured a pool, tennis courts, kennels, and even a dog cemetery. The Brand family cemetery was in the hills farther west. You ride through yet another landfill (goodbye canyon) and after 17 minutes, at mile 0.36, you begin riding on dirt.

At mile 0.42 you keep going left at the junction marked by the signs BRAND and BRAND LAT. This is a very hard climb until the road levels off at 1.67 miles. At 1.76 miles, after 1½ hours, you come to a plateau and a junction with Beaudry Road.

This 2600-foot spot is a good place to stop and relax on the bench provided. You can contemplate the views of Los Angeles, Glendale, Burbank and Griffith Park. From here you take the road that goes to the right and down. At 2.03 miles turn left at the sign VERDUGO-BEAUDRY NORTH. At 2.70 miles you come to a tank and a stream.

At 3.21 miles, after 1:56, you come to another gate, which is difficult to get around, and the end of the dirt. From here you turn right onto paved Beaudry Blvd. At 3.43 miles you turn right onto Country Club Drive. Continue on Country Club even as it curves left. At 3.67 miles, at the signal, turn right onto Canada Blvd.

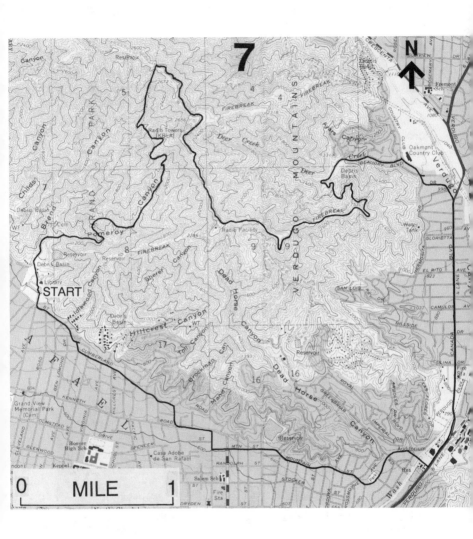

You continue on Canada, pass a small market, and then at 4.51 miles at the first signal past Verdugo Park turn right onto Mountain Street. Continue descending on Mountain until, at 600 feet, it ends at 5.31 miles. Here you turn right onto Central. Almost immediately Central ends, and you turn left onto Kenneth Road at 5.36 miles.

Notice the house at 727 Kenneth. This is "Bel Aire," built by Mattison Boyd Jones, a Los Angeles lawyer, in 1927 and used in many movies, T.V. shows, and commercials. Just past Bel Aire, you turn right onto Valley View Road and then after 2 short blocks, you turn left onto Cumberland Road. Stay on Cumberland until it ends, turn right onto Ard Eevin Avenue and then immediately left onto Mountain Street, and after 6.43 miles and 2¾ hours you are back at the park.

Brand's castle

Trip 8

Beaudry Canyon

Distance: 16.52 miles
Time: 3¼ hours
Elevation gain: 2000 feet
Difficulty: Strenuous
Topo: Burbank, Pasadena
Thomas Bros map: page 8, section E4

In 1870, when Rancho Verdugo was split up, 1702 acres were awarded to Prudent Beaudry. Two years later, after promising to spend $200 in gold coin to prospect for coal, he was given an additional 30 acres on the west bank of the Arroyo in what is today the San Rafael area of Pasadena. In 1876, in order to carry out this agreement, he dug a mine shaft and recovered about one ton of coal. But it was only a pocket, and no more was recovered. Then this shaft was expanded into a tunnel by Samuel Carson, Kit Carson's son. The tunnel provided access to and from Los Angeles without going over the Avenue 64 hill and provided water to the Garvanza district of Los Angeles. Dirt excavated from the tunnel probably either created or increased Beaudry Lake. The tunnel was considered extremely dangerous, and in 1923 it was replaced by a cut known as Beaudry's Cut.

Today, Beaudry's name is virtually unknown in Pasadena. The lake remains but is known as Johnson Lake. And the cut remains but is paved and known as Burleigh Drive. However, in the Glendale area, Beaudry has several roads, paved and unpaved, named after him.

You park, at 1200 feet, on Beaudry Blvd. and begin riding up extremely steep Beaudry Lane. At mile 0.09 you go around a gate. It is difficult to lift a bike over this gate. I had to put the bike through the bars of the gate.

At mile 0.45 you turn left onto the road by the BEAUDRY S. BEAUDRY N. sign. Most people will tell you that the "S." stands for south and the "N." stands for north. This is not true. As you will soon see, the "S." must stand for Steep and the "N." for Not so steep.

All the way up this canyon, you get glimpses of the San Gabriels. Then, at mile 0.93, after 20 minutes of climbing, you come to a plateau from which your view includes Mt. Lukens, Strawberry Peak, Mt. Wilson, and the Verdugos, including Cerro Negro.

Then, at mile 1.07, you can see from Glendale to downtown Los Angeles and beyond all the way to the ocean. At 1.19 miles is a short downhill but you begin climbing again at 1.35 miles.

At 1.84 miles, after 49 minutes of climbing, you arrive at the first of many false summits. From here you can see Strawberry, Wilson, Baldy, Santiago, San Pedro Harbor, Catalina and Griffith Park, with Glendale in the foreground and Los Angeles in the background. Below you, housing developments can be seen making their slow climb to the top.

At 2.45 miles, after 1 hour of climbing, you come to a junction. One road climbs 1/10 of a mile to a summit, with a microwave tower while another road descends to Glendale. But you keep riding on Beaudry. From this spot you can see Burbank, with Griffith Park, the Santa Monicas, and the San Fernando Valley in the background.

At 2.56 miles there is another summit with a radio tower. In the spring, the road is surrounded by wild mustard, poppies, and an extremely prolific purple plant. At 3.20 miles you come to yet another tower, this one signed KBLA. From here there is a paved but sandy downhill. At 3.56 miles you reach the junction with Beaudry N. If you're tired, you can turn right here and quickly return to the car.

But we continue uphill. After 4.18 miles of climbing and walking, you come to a 2600-foot junction that has a bench. While resting on the bench, you take in the view of downtown Los Angeles, with Burbank and Glendale in the foreground and Griffith Park and the Silver Lake Reservoir in the background.

A short road climbs up to a cistern, while another dirt road descends to Brand Park. A sign has a graffito that says "One Hour Club." I assume that means 1 hour either on a bike or on foot. This is discouraging, because it's taken me 1½ hours to reach this spot.

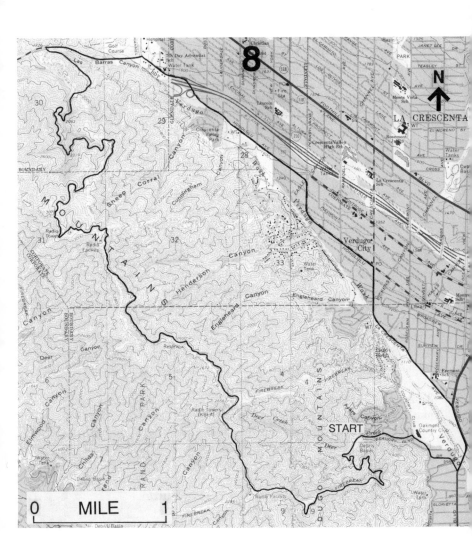

From a distance, this road appears level, but while riding it you keep climbing and climbing to 3000 feet. At 4.48 miles you come to a junction and turn right, and at 5.58 miles you come to a junction signed WHITING, where you ride straight.

At 6.34 miles, after riding past or seeing many more radio transmission towers, you come to a junction signed HOSTELLER. Here you turn right and finally begin descending.

This is a very pleasant descent through chaparral. At 8.94 miles, with Mt. Lukens in the background, you pass some commercial bee hives. You hit pavement and then at 9.43 miles, after 2½ hours, you come to an old fire gate that is no longer used and appears to be perpetually open.

Then you ride past something unexplainable. Here you find a beautifully paved road, complete with double yellow center lines, curbs and manhole covers. On the side of the road is a small but elaborate wooden cross. But the road goes nowhere. And it is closed to most traffic. At 9.90 miles you reach a new fire gate, which restricts access to this mysteriously paved road. Was it to be a subdivision? To add to the mystery, all along the fence that further blocks access to the paved road are red flags. Why?

Here you turn right onto unsigned La Tuna Canyon Road and ride under the freeway. After a short climb paralleling the freeway, you pedal easily downhill to 1600 feet, until at 11.23 miles you turn right onto Honolulu Avenue. Now the ride becomes very satisfying, because in a few minutes you ride from "Honolulu" to "Boston" to "New York."

At 12.83 miles you come to an intersection that has a small market. Here you turn right onto Pennsylvania Avenue, which soon becomes Honolulu again. At 13.76 miles you turn right onto La Crescenta. This becomes Verdugo Road and at 15.56 miles and 1000 feet you turn right onto Country Club Drive and begin your climb back to our start. At 16.06 miles you turn left onto Beaudry and at 16.52 miles you are back at the start, after 3¼ hours.

Trip 9

Stough Canyon

Distance: 10.91 miles
Time: 2 hours
Elevation gain: 1500 feet
Difficulty: Moderate
Topo: Burbank
Thomas Bros map: page 17, section E2
Other family activities: Stough Park playground and golf course.

This ride starts at the 1240-foot top of Walnut Avenue in Burbank's Stough Park. You carry your bike over or under the gate and begin riding up the pavement, which ends at mile 0.20. This is right next to a golf course, and it is a good idea to keep your helmet on to avoid being beaned by an inaccurate golfer. At mile 0.82 you go right.

At 1.17 miles you have a view to the right of the Burbank/Glendale area, with Griffith Park and downtown Los Angeles in the background. After a half-hour of riding you reach a 2080-foot saddle at 1.40 miles. From there you can see the 210 freeway and the San Gabriel Mountains' Big Tujunga Canyon straight ahead. After turning left, the road levels out until at 1.87 miles you have a good view of the Monterey Hills, downtown Los Angeles, Griffith Park, the Santa Monica Mountains, Santa Susana Pass, and Mt. Lukens. In front of you are Burbank and the Burbank airport. Some amazing planes were developed at the Lockheed plant, located at the airport, including the P-38 Lightning, the F-104, the U-2, and the Stealth Fighter. These days you can observe the incredibly steep landings and take-offs that commercial flights are required to make in order to use this airport.

You descend and then climb again several times. This is an area which seems to be especially teeming with deer. Is it because the freeway has cut the deer off from their natural predators or because no hunting is allowed in these hills? Whatever the reason, the canyons are laced with deer trails.

At 4.78 miles, after one hour of riding, you begin to notice graffiti and increasing amounts of broken bottles. Then you go around a gate onto paved Edmore Place. At 4.95 miles turn right on Lanark Street and descend on Lanark, turning left at the light onto Glenoaks Blvd. At the stoplight after the liquor store at 6.74 miles, after a descent to 700 feet, you turn left onto Buena Vista Street and then right, at the first street, onto Kenneth Road. You turn left onto University Avenue at 8.28 miles. At the end of University, turn right onto Bel Aire Drive and then make an immediate left around the gate posted RESTRICTED ENTRY: NO MOTORCYCLES, NO MOTOR SCOOTERS, NO MOTOR VEHICLES.

Now you slowly make one hairpin turn after another as you climb up the hill. Pass the Burbank wood lot, and then at 10.20 miles you go around a gate and turn right onto paved Lockheed View Drive. At the end of Lockheed, you turn left onto Walnut Avenue and you return to the start at 10.91 miles after 2 hours of riding.

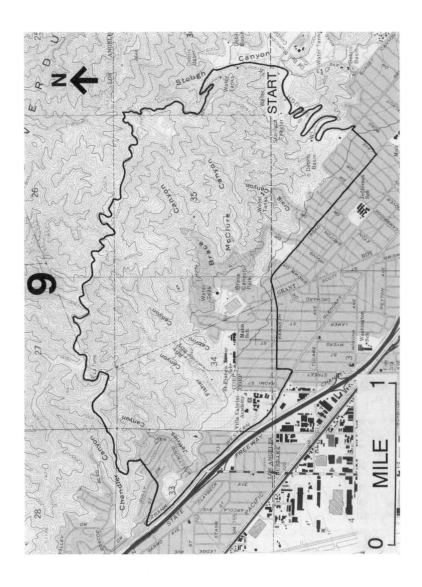

Trip 10

Mission Peak

Distance: 6.32 miles
Time: 2¼ hours
Elevation gain: 1500 feet
Difficulty: Strenuous
Topo: Oat Mountain
Thomas Bros map: page 127, section D3

This trip starts in Granada Hills at the end of Neon Way, at 1500 feet above sea level. You lift your bike over the gate and start climbing this route, which a sign identifies as the DR. MARIO A. DECAMPOS TRAIL.

You climb through hills, which in the spring are covered with shoulder-height wild mustard, and you may also be able to hear a stream that flows to your right. Beginning at mile 0.15, you pass through several sets of gates, which appear to be permanently open.

At 2.11 miles, just past a hitching post, you make a sharp left and at 2.24 miles, after climbing for an hour you reach the 2771-foot summit of Mission Peak. One of my earliest memories is driving up here with my grandfather in a 1946 Ford woody wagon and looking out over, not an endless sea of tract houses, but the open countryside of the San Fernando Valley of the late Forties.

My grandfather told me (incorrectly) that this was the highest point in the City of Los Angeles. Mount Lukens may be technically higher, but Mission Peak's height still produces an almost 360° view. Beyond the houses one can see Griffith Park, the Santa Monicas,

Santa Susana Pass, the unspoiled country toward Newhall, nearby Bee Canyon, the San Gabriels, Hansen Dam, and the Verdugos.

A marker on Mission Peak is "dedicated to [Mario A. DeCampos M.D.] . . . our friend and colleague who loved mountain climbing and cherished Mission Peak."

Several years ago, a fire swept this summit, but the beauty is slowly returning. Poppies, mustard, and even a few yuccas are beginning to reappear.

On the way down, just past the gate at 2.96 miles, you turn left onto a smaller, less-travelled dirt road. In places this is an extremely steep descent. And you can expect to meet hikers, as you are now riding in O'Melveny Park. As you descend into it, you encounter spectacular views of Bee Canyon and at 4.35 miles, well into the park, you come to a drinking fountain.

At 4.57 miles you turn right and cross a wooden bridge, which in the spring spans a flowing stream. At 4.96 miles is another drinking fountain.

You keep riding downhill until at 5.58 miles, at 1340 feet, in the parking lot for the park, you turn right at the wooden O'MELVENY PARK sign and cross the small wooden pedestrian bridge. You turn right onto Meadowlark Avenue, which immediately becomes Sesnon Blvd. At 6.10 miles you turn right onto Neon Ave and at 6.32 miles, after 2¼ hours you return to the start.

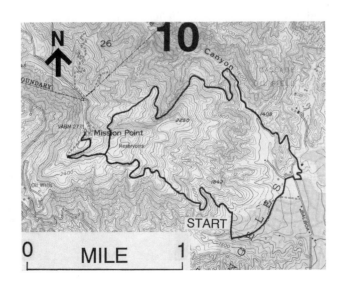

Trip 11

Limekiln Canyon

Distance: 4.01 miles
Time: 1 hour
Elevation gain: 400 feet
Difficulty: Easy
Topo: Oat Mountain
Thomas Bros map: page 7, section 1A

This ride begins in the Porter Ranch section of the City of Los Angeles, at 1100 feet, at the end of Rinaldi Street, ¼ mile west of its intersection with Tampa Avenue. There's a gate at the end of Rinaldi with a NO TRESPASSING sign on one side and a RESTRICTED ENTRY, NO MOTORCYCLES sign on the other. We're going to avoid this contradiction by turning right onto the paved path and going around the gate to the right to enter Limekiln Canyon Park.

At mile 0.10 the road turns to dirt and at mile 0.20 you cross a bridge and ride through a green, grassy section of the park with many planted pine trees. At mile 0.35 you ford the main stream in Limekiln Canyon and at mile 0.50 you ford a smaller stream that feeds into it.

At mile 0.68 you take the road to the right, which becomes very steep, and at mile 0.89 you ride underneath a new, huge, concrete bridge. You can see a small waterfall to your left which has been created as the water from the stream falls over the sloppy concrete left underneath the bridge.

You climb until at mile 0.95 you are separated from Tampa only by a sidewalk and a wooden hitching post/railing. You again descend into the canyon, and at 1.43 miles you turn left onto a partly paved road. At 1.74 miles, by the ALISO CANYON TRAIL, MOONSHINE CANYON TRAIL sign, you go left onto an old, paved road. When this road ends at 1.91 miles, you push your bike up the steep path onto Sesnon Blvd., reaching it in 45 minutes. Here at 1425 feet, you turn right onto Sesnon and then immediately right onto Tampa. Descend until at 3.81 miles you come to the intersection of Tampa and Rinaldi, where there are a market, a fast-food restaurant, and a liquor store.

Turn right onto Rinaldi and return to the start at 4.01 miles after 1 hour.

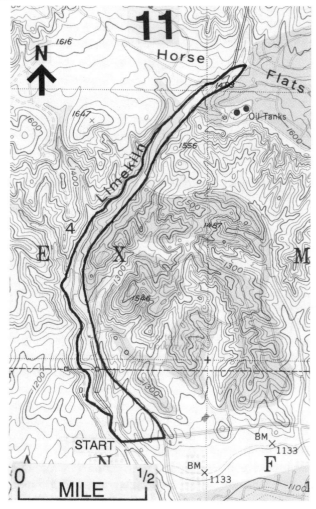

Trip 12

Limekiln-Aliso Canyons

Distance: 6.89 miles
Time: 1½ hours
Elevation gain: 500 feet
Difficulty: Easy
Topo: Oat Mountain
Thomas Bros map: page 7, section A1

To do this ride you take Trip 11 until, after 45 minutes, you turn left onto Tampa and take it to the end. There you take the signed equestrian trail to the right. At 2.39 miles, after climbing to 1600 feet in back of some tract homes, you turn right onto unsigned Ormskirk Ave.

At 2.67 miles, after passing Porter Ridge Park, which has water, you turn left onto Kirkcolm Lane and then immediately left onto Sesnon. Continue riding along Sesnon until it ends at 3.03 miles. Here you go left around a gate onto a dirt road and descend to 1400 feet in Aliso Canyon. At 3.35 miles you go right onto a smaller dirt road and ride down next to Aliso Canyon Creek. Here the main equestrian trail ascends, but you stay on the single track.

At 3.52 miles runoff from the lawns and streets of a housing development flows into the creekbed, and at 3.73 miles you come to a short section of trail that is badly eroded, forcing you to dismount and carefully walk your bike.

At 3.80 miles you cross a streambed and continue on the single track, which soon widens into an equestrian trail. At 3.96 miles and at 4.05 miles you cross the streambed. At 4.49 miles take the left fork and at 4.89 miles turn right onto Rinaldi. Although a major paved thoroughfare, it is elevated enough that it gives you an excellent view of the San Fernando Valley and the entire Santa Monicas from Griffith Park to the Santa Susanas.

At 6.64 miles you come to the intersection with Tampa, where you will find a market, a fast-food restaurant, and a liquor store. Then, at 6.89 miles and after 1½ hours, you are back at the start.

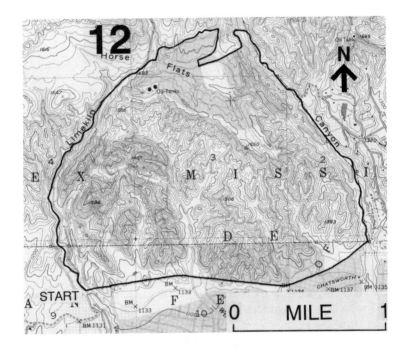

Trip 13

Mulholland

Distance: 25.64 miles
Time: 5 hours
Elevation gain: 2500 feet
Difficulty: Strenuous
Topo: Beverly Hills, Canoga Park, Topanga, Van Nuys
Thomas Bros map: page 22, section B6

This ride starts from the 1190-foot Park & Ride lot on Rimerton Road next to the San Diego Freeway at the Mulholland Drive exit. This is a very small Park & Ride, especially considering the amount of traffic that the San Diego freeway carries. Yet, it has four phone booths, which always seem to be busy. There is a constant roar from the freeway, and the traffic seems to be heavy any time of the day or night.

You leave the lot and turn left onto Rimerton. At mile 0.33 you turn left onto Mulholland Drive and begin a gradual climb. At mile 0.91 the road levels off and, if you've chosen a clear day, you get a view of the San Fernando Valley.

At 1.54 miles is the Fryman Canyon Overlook Lookout. At the stop sign at 1.74 miles most vehicles go to the right onto Calneva Drive, but you continue straight on unsigned Mulholland.

Just past Stone Oak Drive, after 2.00 miles, nearly all traffic has disappeared, and even though the road is paved, you essentially have it to yourself, and can hear birds, insects and other sounds of nature for the first time.

At 2.38 miles at the sign, ENCINO HILLS DRIVE—MULHOLLAND DRIVE, Mulholland turns left. Although technically paved, this section is badly eroded and you have essentially entered the off-road world.

You soon pass a strange concrete blockhouse, but the thing that catches your eye is the enormous amounts of trash that people have dumped here. One peculiarity is the number of concrete blocks, the kind that were used for board-and-block bookcases by financially strapped tenants in the 1960s. And instead of being dumped in one spot, they have been scattered for almost a mile. Fortunately, the farther you ride, the less trash you encounter.

At 3.30 miles, after 45 minutes you have an excellent view of the Encino Reservoir, which local residents call Lake Encino. At 3.49 miles is an entrance to one of the many dirt fireroads that take off from Mulholland. This one has several radio antennas and what appears to be an old radar support tower from an abandoned Nike missile base.

At 4.42 miles you come to another overlook with an excellent view of Lake Encino and the San Fernando Valley to the north, and more of the Santa Monica Mountains to the south.

This is an extremely bumpy road, even when slowly climbing uphill. Since it's open to traffic, you will encounter a few motorcycles and 4×4's, most of them going too fast. Fortunately, you can hear them long before they reach you. At 6.09 miles you pass a trail on your left, signed NO BIKES, which goes into Topanga State Park.

For the second time you climb to 1900 feet, with excellent views of both the almost completely developed San Fernando Valley and the almost completely undeveloped Santa Monica Mountains. Then you encounter a downhill section with sand so white, you could be at Cancun, Mexico.

At 7.57 miles you come to a fenced reservoir. If you are lucky enough to find the gates open, you can get water from the faucet inside the fence.

After 2 hours you have descended to 1503 feet and you turn left onto paved Santa Maria Road, marked by three signs: SANTA MARIA ROAD, SANTA MONICA MOUNTAIN CONSERVANCY, and FAIR HILLS FARMS ONE MILE.

As you descend, you pass several small-to-large rural ranches. On your left, you'll see an interesting sandstone formation, and then you'll begin an extremely steep climb. You are rewarded, at 10.41

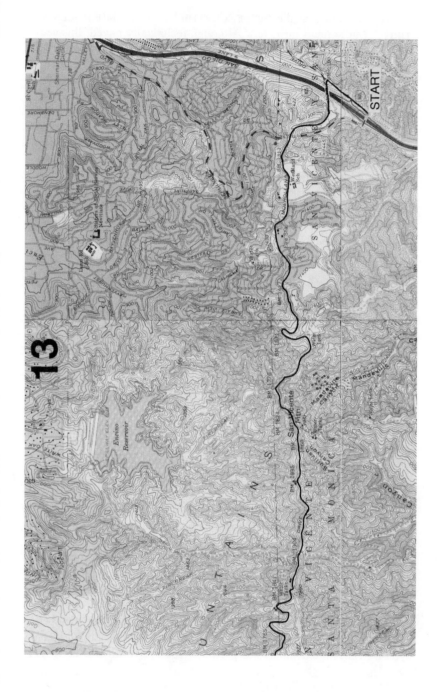

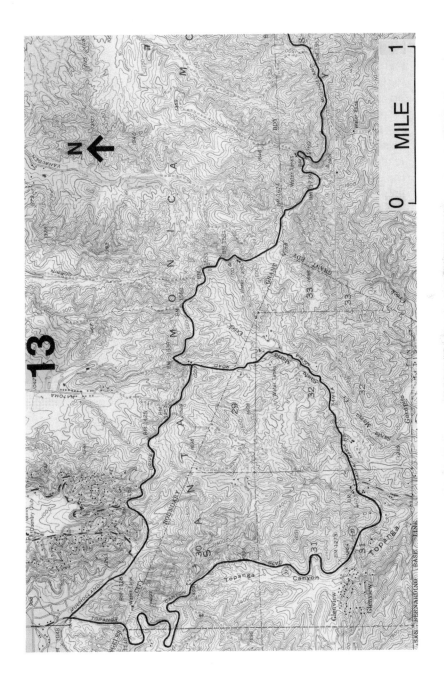

miles, by a fabulous, steep, paved descent. With its twists and turns, it feels just like you're on a roller coaster.

At 10.78 miles, after 2½ hours, you've dropped almost to 1000 feet, and you turn right onto Topanga Canyon Blvd. This is the tip of the old, fast-disappearing, "funky" Topanga. Behind the fence on the other side of the road is a Nash Metropolitan automobile waiting to be rescued.

This can be a hot ride, but you can also occasionally catch a cool ocean breeze in the late afternoon. At 12.78 miles, after 3 hours, you reach the 1500-foot summit of Topanga Canyon. To your right, there is a mobile-home park, with some homes looking out directly over an area signed WARNING SEWER EFFLUENT.

You descend, until just past the 11.00 milepost, at 1014 feet and 14.59 miles, you reach Mulholland Drive. (An additional ½ mile descent on Topanga takes you to a small shopping center with a market, doughnuts, pizza, a deli, etc.) Turn right, but instead of taking paved Mulholland which is quite narrow at this point, ride up onto the path on the dirt embankment to the right of the street. In a block, this embankment becomes a divider between the two paved Mulhollands.

At 15.18 miles, at Canoga Avenue, jog right onto the paved, but unsigned Mulholland which has a PAVEMENT ENDS 1200 FT. sign. Do not take the "signed" Mulholland, which parallels it, has a DEAD END sign, and is blocked by a wrought iron gate. At 15.56 miles the pavement ends. At 16.77 miles, after 3½ hours, you again come to the junction with Santa Maria Road.

At 23.30 miles you turn right and leave the unpaved section of Mulholland. From here you can almost coast back to the start. At 25.31 miles you cross the San Diego Freeway and turn right and at 25.64 miles, after 5 hours, you are back at the Park & Ride lot.

Trip 14

Overlook

Distance: 10.16 miles
Time: 2¼ hours
Elevation gain: 1000 feet
Difficulty: Moderate to strenuous
Topo: Point Mugu
Thomas Bros map: Ventura County, page 81A, section B6
Other family activities: Swimming and other beach activities at Sycamore Cove State Beach.

When I first started mountain biking in Point Mugu State Park, this canyon was a real surprise to me. I had driven and cycled by here many times on the Pacific Coast Highway. I had even camped a few times at the cyclists' campground, but I had never taken the time to explore the other world that exists just a few hundred yards away from the highway.

You can pay to park in the state park or leave your car on the Pacific Coast Highway. During the week and on winter weekends you can probably park, at just 20 feet above sea level, on the triangular dirt area just outside the entrance. On a summer weekend you'll probably have to park farther away on the Pacific Coast Highway. Just notice the many no-parking signs: some are NO PARKING 10PM TO 5AM but others are NO PARKING ANY TIME.

As you ride into the park, you pass a huge bougainvillea tree just before the entrance, and at mile 0.07 you come to a drinking fountain and restrooms. After filling your water bottles here, you ride through the campground.

At mile 0.21 you go around the gate and onto a dirt road signed SYCAMORE CANYON TRAIL. There is a no-motorcycles sign, which at a glance looks almost like a no-bicycles sign.

Immediately you notice a sign with many strictures. You can probably correctly conclude from this sign that access by mountain bike could easily be prohibited in the future.

Also notice the SCENIC TRAIL sign to your left, which is posted no bikes. An irony of all the *no-bicycles* signs is that due to the popularity of mountain bicycles, you'll find many more cyclists here than hikers or equestrians.

At mile 0.63 you come to the first of many fire hydrants, most of which have a spigot so you can get drinking water. At mile 0.73 you pass the junction with the OVERLOOK TRAIL road. You will return that way, but for now keep going straight. At 1.06 miles you come to the Overlook Hiking Trail, which is posted NO BIKES.

At mile 1.35 you come to another trail posted NO BIKES and another source of water. Then at 2.27 miles, after 30 minutes, you find a few wooden picnic tables, under the shade of some enormous, old oak trees. At 2.84 miles you encounter a slight uphill, and then at 3.28 miles, after 45 minutes, you come to another water faucet at the 209-foot junction of the Wood Canyon and Sycamore Canyon roads, where you go left.

At 3.98 miles you reach another source of water and at 4.04 miles, after an hour of riding, you turn left onto Overlook at the junction of the Overlook and Wood Canyon roads. This section is beyond steep, gaining 600 feet in just ¾ of a mile; it has the nickname of "Hell Hill." At 4.79 miles, after 1¼ hours of riding and walking, the Overlook Trail turns left. At 5.09 miles, after 1½ hours of climbing, the road continues to climb, but not as steeply, and gives you an excellent view up Sycamore Canyon.

From the 1000-foot summit of the road at 5.60 miles, you can see La Jolla Valley (to your left), upper Sycamore Canyon, some of the beautiful rock formations for which the Santa Monica Mountains are famous and, on a clear day in the distance, the San Gabriels.

At 6.10 miles, after 1¾ hours, you have your first view of the Pacific since the start, and at 6.68 miles you look down upon the surf and the park's La Jolla Beach Campground.

From a point at 8.79 miles you can see Sycamore Canyon Beach, the Pacific Coast Highway, and a rock formation on the other side of the highway. At 9.43 miles turn right onto Sycamore Canyon Road, and at 9.86 miles you re-enter the campground. At 10.16 miles, after 2¼ hours of cycling, you are back at the start.

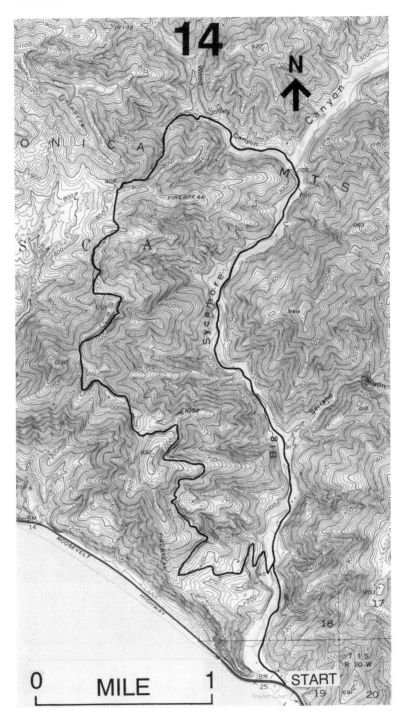

Trip 15

Sycamore Canyon

Distance: 15.50 miles
Time: 2¾ hours
Elevation gain: 800 feet
Difficulty: Easy, with one moderate climb
Topo: Point Mugu, Triunfo Pass, Newbury Park
Thomas Bros map: Ventura County, page 81A, section B6
Other family activities: Swimming and other beach activities at Sycamore Cove State Beach.

In 1542, when Portuguese explorer Juan Rodriguez Cabrillo first "discovered" this coast, the Chumash Indians had been living here for 6000 years. In fact, the word "Mugu" comes from a Chumash word, "muwu," which meant beach. In 1846 Governor Pio Pico granted 36,000 acres in the Point Mugu area to Isabel Maria Yorba, who sold 22,000 acres in 1873 to William Broome. In 1966 the state purchased the land from the Broome family.

This ride follows the same route as Trip 14 until at 3.28 miles after 45 minutes you come to the water faucet at the junction of the Wood Canyon and Sycamore Canyon roads, where you go right.

You ride through a large meadow, with the streambed on your left, and then cross the streambed and pass an old barn and corral. At 4.56 miles you keep going straight on the Big Sycamore Canyon Trail following the TO RANCH CENTER ROAD sign. Now you ride through the streambed again, and then at 4.90 miles you go left onto pavement.

At 5.33 miles, after 65 minutes of riding, you come to the Sycamore Multi-Use area, an equestrian center, with port-a-potties, picnic tables, corrals, a faucet, and a slimy water trough. I usually complain about water being available only for horses, and not for cyclists, but I wouldn't want even my horse to drink from this one.

At 5.74 miles you continue riding straight on the paved road. At 6.55 miles there is water on the right. Then you cross a bridge and from an elevation of 500 feet you begin climbing. While you're struggling up the hill, don't fail to look up to your right and see the interesting rock formations on the other side of the canyon.

At 7.42 miles you reach the 872-foot summit, from which you can see from the distant San Gabriels to the rock formation on your right. At 7.51 miles you come to the State Park boundary and at 7.71 miles you turn onto the trail to your right. At 7.75 miles, after 1¼ hours, you reach a rest area near the Satwiwa cultural center, which has been open Sundays since June 1983. The rest area features shade, water, picnic tables, and some exhibits about the area and its former Native American residents.

Return the way you came, reaching the start at 15.50 miles after 2¾ hours of riding.

Except for lack of snow, Sugarloaf Peak looks like the Paramount logo

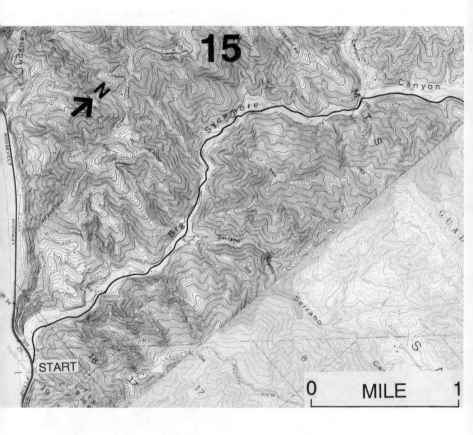

Trip 16

Paramount Ranch

Distance: 3.54 miles
Time: 1 hour
Elevation gain: 150 feet
Difficulty: Easy, with some moderate hills
Topo: Malibu Beach, Point Dume
Thomas Bros map: Page 100A, section B6
Other family activities: Western town, nature hike

In the late Teens and early Twenties, Jesse Lasky, a co-owner of Paramount Pictures, realized that his company had outgrown its Burbank studios. They had become too crowded, and because of the limited shooting sites, all of Paramount's films were beginning to look alike.

So in 1921 he bought 4000 acres of the old Rancho Las Virgenes in Agoura. It served as San Francisco for *Wells Fargo*, the Orient for *The Adventures of Marco Polo*, and the Mississippi River environs for *Tom Sawyer*. So much shooting was done that permanent metal storage sheds were built.

Then times changed, and in 1946 Paramount sold the property. In 1952 Bill Hertz, a western movie buff, bought the 326 acres that contained the warehouses. Hertz purchased some old western sets from Twentieth Century Fox and converted the former warehouses into a fantasy western town.

In the 1950s the town became the location for many television shows including *The Cisco Kid*, *Bat Masterson*, *The Zane Grey Theater*, and *Have Gun Will Travel*. Later, *The Fall Guy*, *Reds*,

Chips, BJ and the Bear, and *Helter Skelter* were filmed here. Today it is still the location for many films, television shows, commercials, and catered picnics.

In 1980 the National Park Service purchased the ranch and made it a part of the Santa Monica Mountains National Recreational Area. It can be reached via Kanan-Dume Road from either the Pacific Coast Highway or the Ventura Freeway. You turn south from Kanan-Dume onto Cornell Road. This is a little-publicized park, and from Kanan-Dume, the only evidence that Paramount Ranch exists is that the CORNELL ROAD sign is the National Park Service brown and white rather than the usual green and white. After entering the park, you go left ⅛ mile and start the ride near the bridge that allows entry into the western town.

From this 760-foot spot, instead of crossing the bridge, you head south following the hard-to-find RUN TRAIL sign at the end of the wooden fence. At the oak tree at mile 0.07 you bear right and then immediately either ride around or lift your bike over a barrier. At the first junction, at mile 0.17, you turn left onto a single track and begin climbing above and parallel to Mulholland Highway.

You go left at the junction near the top of the hill and then attain the 800-foot summit at mile 0.43 after 9 minutes of fairly hard work. From here you can see the western town and the surrounding Santa Monicas, but your view is dominated by Sugarloaf Mountain, which except for the lack of snow looks exactly like the peak Paramount uses in their logo.

After absorbing the view, you descend and at mile 0.54 you begin riding along the fence that parallels Cornell Road until at mile 0.62, by the gate onto Mulholland, you turn left.

After passing a house, you go right at the junction at mile 0.78. Back at the parking lot at mile 0.89, you go left onto some old asphalt. In the sports-car-crazy 1950s, a racetrack was built here. It was also used in many films including some of the "Herbie, the Love Bug" series. Presumably the surface has severely eroded in the intervening thirty years, because this would be one tough track to drive in a 1950s sports car. The former track curves to the right and passes some exposed layers of sedimentary rocks.

The asphalt ends next to a large oak tree, and after 20 minutes you're back at the parking lot again. You ride through the parking lot and pass the "official" start/finish line. Follow the old racetrack once more, past the entrance from Cornell Road, to a point where barriers make further use of the racetrack impossible. Here you turn left onto the signed trail. At 1.68 miles, bear right onto the asphalt again, until at 1.76 miles you leave the asphalt and ride left onto a dirt road. Just before Cornell Road, the dirt road swings right and parallels the park boundary.

At 2.05 miles you pass through a fence that is posted NO HORSES. At 2.29 miles, after 34 minutes you find yourself back at the parking lot. Turn left, and then make a right at 2.35 miles. You enter the shade of some creekside trees, parallel Medea Creek for a short ways, and then cross the creek by riding through it.

You leave the shelter of the trees and turn left onto a wide, eroded asphalt/dirt road. At the sign at 2.55 miles, go left and follow the trail, which passes through a wooden fence on the right. You veer to the right of the old raceway and ride onto a single track. Then you turn left onto the raceway and begin riding it again, until in the middle of a banked left-hand turn, you turn right onto a dirt area near the western town.

From here you turn sharply to the right and take the single track, signed COYOTE TRAIL, to the right of the huge oak tree by the old cabin and begin climbing. At 2.97 miles you keep right and at 3.10 miles you turn left and climb to the 700-foot picnic area. From the picnic area, which is reached after 51 minutes, you can just make out Malibu Lake to the south. Descend and turn left onto the main trail again. At 3.35 miles you're back at the racetrack again. This time you ride through the western town.

After a quick look, this appears to be one old town. However, a more thorough inspection reveals that the "glass" windows are actually plastic and that all the wood, stone, and brick siding is actually fiberglass. The town has both water and restrooms.

Then you leave the town, cross the Medea Creek bridge and reach the start at 3.54 miles, after one hour.

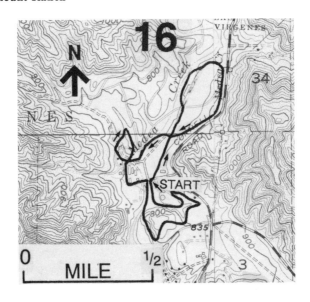

Author riding through "old" Western town in Paramount Ranch

Trip 17

Malibu Creek

Distance: 9.30 miles
Time: 1 ¾ hours
Elevation gain: 550 feet
Difficulty: Moderate
Topo: Malibu Beach, Point Dume
Thomas Bros map: Page 107, section E4
Other family activities: Nature trail, visitor center, hikes

On this ride you will keep finding yourself thinking, "I've been here before." That's because, until 1974, much of this land was owned by 20th Century Fox, and many movies and television programs were shot here, including "The Planet of the Apes." The park's many beautiful rock formations have served as backdrops for thousands of productions. You'll ride through the area featured in the opening sequence of the "M*A*S*H" television series. And even though the land is now owned by the state, there is still a lot of location work done here, especially on weekdays, and you may find your ride temporarily halted by a film crew until the shooting of a scene is finished.

Malibu Creek State Park is on Las Virgenes Road 0.3 mile south of Mulholland Highway. You can drive into the park and pay a $3 entrance fee or you can park on the dirt area at the intersection of Las Virgenes and Mulholland and ride into the park.

The ride begins ¼ mile from the entrance station, at the parking lot by the third set of restrooms, the ones with the information kiosks. Leaving this 525-foot area, you ride downhill, cross the main paved road and ride onto paved Crags Road marked by a TRAIL sign.

You immediately cross a bridge over year-round Las Virgenes Creek.

At mile 0.25 the pavement ends, and at the junction at mile 0.44 you go left. You ride through one of the park's many grassland areas, which is dotted with oak trees. Many of the oaks were living when the Spaniards first arrived. You soon come to a picnic area, some more information kiosks, and the visitor center (open weekends), and then cross a bridge over Malibu Creek and continue straight.

At mile 0.91 you turn left onto the trail signed ROCK POOL TRAIL. Soon you reach the rock pools, which have huge boulders in a reflecting pool. This too has been the site of many movies and television shows. Return the way you came, turning left once more onto Crags Road.

At the junction at 1.45 miles keep straight on the road signed TO CENTURY LAKE and begin climbing. At the 725-foot summit, just past the trail signed NO BIKES, you can see the dam for Century Lake, which was built at the turn of the century by affluent members of the exclusive Crags Country Club.

From the summit, you descend to 660 feet, and then at 1.80 miles there is a drinking fountain and you cross Malibu Creek once more. If you stop on the bridge and climb the railing on the south side, you get a view of 7-acre Century Lake, with the rock formations known as Goat Buttes, created by volcanoes millions of years ago, in the background.

Next you ride through an area almost completely shaded by oak and other trees, and although you're still on a fireroad, one side is so rough that it is essentially a single track. At 2.51 miles after 45 minutes, you reach the area where part of the M*A*S*H TV series was filmed. The original set is in the Smithsonian, but an old burned out Jeep and an ambulance remain.

At 2.76 miles you stay right where Bulldog Road takes off to the left, and at 3.05 miles at an unsigned junction (with a manhole cover) you go left. The road to the right dead-ends in ¼ mile at the dam of very private Malibu Lake, but there are some beautiful reflecting pools below the dam.

At 3.12 miles there is a short section of pavement, and then the road begins to climb. At 3.33 miles, after 1 hour of riding, you come to a gate, which you go around and begin cycling on unsigned but now paved Crags Road. After a moderately steep climb, you come to an 825-foot summit at 3.47 miles. You descend, until at 4.01 miles you go right on Lake Vista Drive and begin cycling past Malibu Lake, which has so many NO TRESPASSING signs that they almost detract from its beauty.

At 5.20 miles you turn right onto Mulholland Highway and then at 8.26 miles, just before the SIGNAL AHEAD sign, notice the Sepulveda Adobe on your left. When it was built, Lincoln was President. Here you turn right onto a trail signed CRAGS RD. 0.7M.

(If this trail is closed because of fire hazard, you can continue on Mulholland, turn right onto Las Virgenes, and then right again in 0.3 mile into the park.)

At 8.63 miles you can see the parking lot directly ahead, but the trail, which passes through a field of anise, turns to the right and becomes so extremely steep and unridable that I had to walk. At 9.05 miles you reach Crags Road and turn left. Then at 9.30 miles, after 1¾ hours, you reach the start.

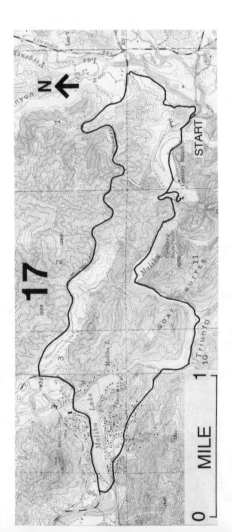

Trip 18

Bulldog Loop

Distance: 14.33 miles
Time: 4½ hours
Elevation gain: 2200 feet
Difficulty: Strenuous
Topo: Malibu Beach, Point Dume
Thomas Bros map: Page 107, section E4
Other family activities: Nature trail, visitor center, hikes

This trip allows you to ride through almost all of Malibu Creek State Park and then climb to see truly spectacular views, from the San Gabriel Mountains to the sea.

This ride follows the same route as Trip 17 until at 2.76 miles, after almost an hour of riding, you turn left onto Bulldog Road and begin climbing. There are some short, steep climbs and some short, steep descents, until at 3.13 miles you come to a fence where you carry your bike over a motorcycle barrier constructed with railroad ties. At the junction at 3.91 miles go left. At 4.25 miles you come to a false summit with great views of Malibu Creek State Park, the rest of the Santa Monicas and even Canyon Country in the distance.

The sharp right turn that the road makes at 5.17 miles is another great place to take a break from this climb and absorb the view. At 6.26 miles, at the 2400-foot junction signed BULLDOG MOTORWAY, notice the interesting rock formations above you and then turn left.

This section of the ride offers views of Catalina Island, Palos Verdes peninsula, Santa Monica Bay, and the San Gabriels. At 6.74

miles you go right and at 7.01 miles, after 2½ hours of riding, you reach a gate signed CASTRO PEAK M/W. From this gate, notice the trail that leaves to the east (left) from the gravel parking lot at the end of Corral Canyon Road.

You descend to the 2000-foot parking lot and begin climbing this trail. I don't know if any movies have actually ever been shot here, but I kept waiting for the Lone Ranger, Gene Autry, or Hopalong Cassidy to ride out from behind one of the beautifully eroded rock formations that you cycle past.

You turn left by the eucalyptus tree at 7.29 miles, and at 7.47 miles turn left, onto the main road. From the 2100-foot summit at 8.71 miles, after 3 hours, you have a great view down into Malibu Creek State Park, including Malibu Lake and you can even see the old army vehicles at the M*A*S*H site.

At 9.90 miles, after 4 hours, you turn left at the junction with the sign MESA PEAK M/W. At 11.83 miles, just after making the sharp right turn with the chain-link fencing, be sure to go right.

At 12.38 miles you go right, and then left onto Las Virgenes at 12.45 miles. Just after passing the Hindu temple on your right, turn left into the State Park entrance at 14.08 miles. At 14.33 miles, after 4½ hours, you are back at the start.

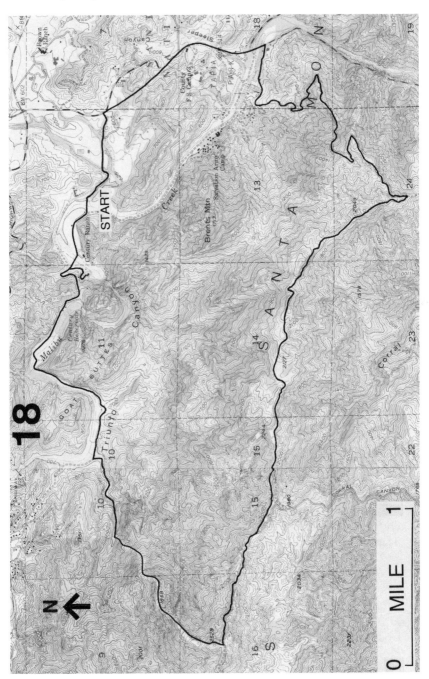

Trip 19

Yellow Hill Road

Distance: 5.80 miles
Time: 2 hours
Elevation gain: 1600 feet
Difficulty: Strenuous
Topo: Triunfo Pass
Thomas Bros map: Page 110, section B3

This ride begins near Leo Carrillo State Beach, at 25 feet above sea level. You park either on the Pacific Coast Highway or on Mulholland Highway. You go around the gate opposite the 0.06 milepost on Mulholland, which is signed YELLOW HILL M/W. Begin climbing, and almost immediately you can see the Pacific Coast Highway, Leo Carrillo beach, and the ocean—but you can also hear the traffic from the highway. The higher you climb, the less noise you can hear, until finally you cannot hear the traffic at all.

At mile 0.64 you look down on Mulholland Highway and Leo Carrillo State Beach's Campground. At 1.47 miles, after 45 minutes of climbing, you reach a gate signed STATE PARK PROPERTY.

Even from here, a spot you assume to be away from any trace of civilization, you can see a building site below you to your right. Then at 1.57 miles you come to another junction. Here you take the middle of the three forks and continue climbing. At 1.80 miles you enter the Santa Monica Mountains National Recreation Area and pass the first of several Department of the Interior boundary signs. To your left is a ranch with horses and a recently planted orchard. Out near the horizon you can spot some of the Channel Islands. Then at 2.33 miles you are high enough to see both Catalina Island and Palos Verdes.

At the YELLOW HILL M/W sign at 2.81 miles, you keep riding straight. At 2.89 miles, after 1¼ hours, you reach a 1600-foot plateau and the outer end of the ride. From this plateau, with the rest of the Santa Monica Mountains behind you, it's possible to see the Channel Islands, Catalina Island, Palos Verdes, and Santa Monica Bay.

Return the same way, reaching the start after 5.80 miles and 2 hours of hard climbing and descending.

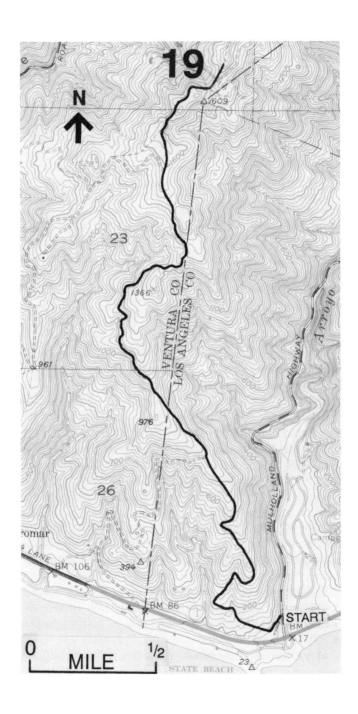

19

N

1609

23

1366

VENTURA CO
LOS ANGELES CO

961

976

26

omar

BM 106

394

BM 86

MULHOLLAND

HIGHWAY

Arroyo

START
BM
17

23

STATE BEACH

0 MILE 1/2

Trip 20

Palos Verdes

Distance: 2.26 miles
Time: 1 hour
Elevation gain: 500 feet
Difficulty: Easy to moderate
Topo: Torrance
Thomas Bros map: Page 77, section E1
Other family activities: Del Cerro Park

Viewed from the San Gabriels on a typical smoggy Southern California day, Palos Verdes appears to be an island rising out of a sea of pollution. But viewed from the Santa Monicas on a clear day, you can see that if the ocean were to rise even slightly, Palos Verdes would actually be another island like Catalina.

Although this ride begins at Del Cerro Park, at the end of Crenshaw Boulevard in Palos Verdes Estates, the park has no restrooms or water, so come prepared.

From the 1180-foot park you ride back to Crenshaw and turn left. Just before the wrought-iron-and-brick fence, you ride up onto the sidewalk on the left side of the road. At mile 0.14, at the beginning of this fence, you turn left onto the dirt path and parallel the fence downhill. At the end of the fence you go through the gate and begin an extremely steep descent down a single track into the canyon (you may want to dismount and walk your bike).

At mile 0.33 you are still descending, but much less steeply. At mile 0.61 you arrive at an 880-foot junction and turn left. At mile 0.68 you turn right, into a clearing and, after absorbing the view from 900 feet above the Pacific, you return to the main trail and continue riding to the right. At mile 0.75 you arrive at a small canyon that requires an uncommonly steep descent to 780 feet (it's even difficult to walk the bike) and then a steep ascent out of it.

At mile 0.90 you turn left onto a fireroad. At 1.20 miles, after 30 minutes, you go right onto a side road and ride out onto a 940-foot knoll with pine trees. From this knoll you have one of the most spectacular views in the Palos Verdes Peninsula. You can see the coast from the former site of Marineland to Portuguese Bend and out to Catalina Island.

Now ride back to the main road, turn right, and then, at 1.62 miles at a four-way junction, go left. You climb and ride past some exposed sedimentary rocks until at 2.11 miles you go around a gate and ride past some bougainvilleas onto the pavement of Crenshaw. At 2.18 miles you turn left into the park, and reach the start at 2.26 miles after one hour of riding.

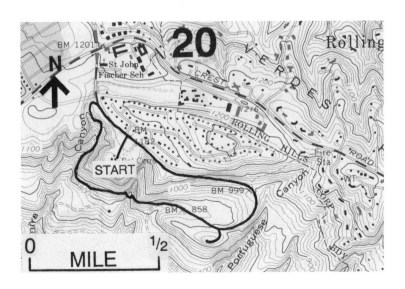

Trip 21

A Whale of a Ride

Distance: 14.91 miles
Time: 3 hours
Elevation gain: 1200 feet
Difficulty: Moderate
Topo: Palos Verdes, San Pedro, Redondo Beach, Torrance
Thomas Bros map: Page 77, section E1
Other family activities: Del Cerro Park, Point Vicente Interpretive Center, Wayfarer's Chapel

Although this ride begins at Del Cerro Park, at the end of Crenshaw Boulevard in Palos Verdes Estates, the park has no restrooms or water, so come prepared. The limited parking in Del Cerro Park means that on weekends you'll need to park on Crenshaw.

From the 1182-foot park you ride back to Crenshaw and turn right. Crenshaw becomes dirt and as you ride between bougainvilleas, you go around or between the crossbars of a gate and begin descending, passing a water tank on your left and an old tower's foundation on your right. Then you pass between some pepper trees and come to a 4-way junction at mile 0.61.

From here you go right, on the main road, and begin a slight ascent as the road continues to curve to the right. At the junction at mile 0.85 you turn left and ride up a little hill to a pine-covered knoll. From the top of this knoll, at mile 0.91, you can see the coast from Marineland to Portuguese Bend (named for Portuguese explorer Juan Rodriguez Cabrillo, who "discovered" this coast in 1542) and out to Catalina Island.

You may wonder why this stretch of California coastline still exists in an undeveloped condition. A sign on Palos Verdes Drive South just south of here gives the answer: PORTUGUESE BEND LANDSLIDE AREA, COASTAL LAND MOVEMENT... USE EXTREME CAUTION. Several homes were lost due to landslides in the mid-Fifties, and even today there are homes on a rather precarious-appearing hill overlooking this sign. In an attempt to prevent further erosion, the hills are laced with large galvanized drain pipes. I can definitely see mountain-bikes being banned from this area because of the possibility of increased erosion, so enjoy the ride while you may.

Do not return to the main road but continue riding on the same trail, which veers left at mile 1.00. At mile 1.38 you come to a 4-way junction. Do not follow the road that parallels the powerline, but turn left. At mile 1.58 you turn left onto the main road and at mile 1.63, just before some yellow pipes, you turn right onto a side road.

Soon you come to a junction near a large water tank, but you continue straight on the same trail. At mile 1.84, where pipes loop out of the ground in a large expansion joint, you turn left. Now you enjoy a nice little downhill, which gives you enough speed to almost take you over the crest of the next hill.

At 2.20 miles veer right, and then at 2.49 miles, after 30 minutes of riding, go right onto paved, unsigned Palos Verdes Drive south. At 2.52 miles a plaque identifies an estate as the former home of Henry E. Benedict (1890–1977) who was one of the co-developers of the original 16,000-acre Palos Verdes Estates.

After 3.13 miles, at milepost 2.45, you turn right and climb the short hill to the Wayfarer's Chapel. It was built in 1951 as a memorial to Emanuel Swedenborg, an 18th-century scientist, philosopher, and theologian. Inspired by the redwood trees of northern California, Lloyd Wright, Frank Lloyd Wright's son and fellow architect, designed this chapel almost entirely of glass. Nearly invisible from the road below, you have the feeling that you are surrounded by trees, not glass. It achieves a tranquillity that another glass church, Anaheim's Crystal Cathedral, only attempts. In the Fifties and Sixties it was "the" spot for many celebrities, and Jayne Mansfield, among others, was married here.

After leaving this very serene spot, you turn right again onto Palos Verdes Drive. At 5.36 miles, after 1 hour of riding, you turn left at the signal into the Point Vicente Interpretive Center.

Just as you are feeling you are light years away from any problems of civilization, you notice a closed parking lot signed DUE

TO INCREASED VANDALISM IN THE PARK THIS AREA HAS BEEN
CLOSED.

At 5.58 miles, after 1 hour of riding, you reach the Interpretive
Center. What this center interprets is the annual, December to April
migration of the California gray whale. This is an excellent spot from
which to view the whales because they hug the coast at this point. In
1989 2415 whales were sighted from this area.

At 5.80 miles you turn right onto unsigned Palos Verdes Drive
once more. Just past the Coast Guard lighthouse, at 5.91 miles, you
engage your lowest gear, go right, and ride over the curb onto a dirt
trail. At 5.99 miles you reach the summit of a small hill, which offers
rewarding views of the coastline from Marineland to the Interpretive Center, You backtrack along the trail, turning right at 6.09 miles
onto the paved highway once more.

At 6.29 miles you pass the Point Vicente Public Fishing
Access—although after you've read the warnings concerning DDT
and PCB, I'm not sure anyone would want to eat anything caught
here. At this point you take the paved bikepath which parallels the
highway. At 6.71 miles, at the end of the bikepath, turn right and ride
into the former Marineland parking lot. At 7.15 miles you reach the
old entrance. The entire place looks like a ghost town; only the ticket
booths and the observation tower remain.

You turn around, retrace your path through the parking lot, and at
7.59 miles, after 1¾ hours of riding you turn right once more onto
Palos Verdes Drive South. You pass Abalone Cove, another beach
access, then at 9.05 miles you pass the entrance to a private estate,
that resembles a Roman villa, and is signed PORTVGVESE POINT.

At 11.88 miles, after 2 hours of riding, you turn right onto a wide
dirt road with a DO NOT ENTER sign for cars. Keep right at the next
two junctions. At 12.09 miles you have reached the end of the road
and can see a good example of what landslides can do. Over the
years, the landslides have ripped and twisted this particular spot into
what could be some artist's conception of the surface of an alien
world.

Returning to Palos Verdes Drive South, you are tempted to
explore where some of the other branches of this road lead. One
leads to a paved road that takes you to a beach which, because of its
palm trees, palm-frond-covered beach shelters, and island off the
coast, reminds me of Hawaii. Unfortunately, it is the private property of the Portuguese Bend Beach Club.

So you return to Palos Verdes Drive South and turn right. At
12.38 miles you carefully cross the highway and begin riding back up

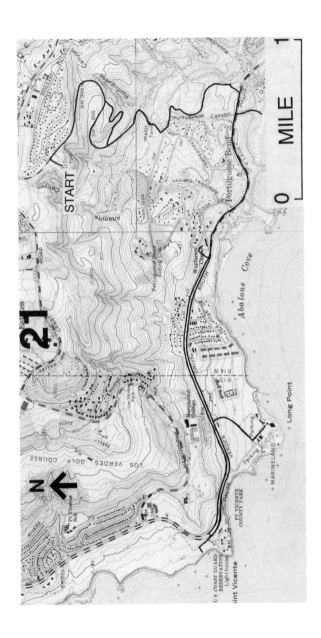

the dirt road. At 12.45 miles veer right at the junction, and at 12.67 miles go left, following the large galvanized pipe. At 13.09 miles you make a right at the **Y** by the telephone pole, and at 13.19 miles, you cross the exposed pipe, by the expansion joint, and go right onto the trail, which becomes a real pusher.

At 13.41 miles turn left onto the main road and at 13.59 miles continue straight at a 4-way junction. You stay on the main road as it curves to the right and skirt the pine-tree-covered knoll. At 14.33 miles go left at a 4-way junction. If you have done this ride in the late afternoon, the view from this last stretch of road, with Catalina in the background, the knoll in the foreground, and the sun setting into the Pacific can be fantastic. You go around the gate once more and at 14.91 miles, after 3 hours of riding, you turn left into Del Cerro Park.

Portuguese Bend seen from the Whale ride

Trip 22

Baldwin Hills

Distance: 0.72 mile
Time: 20 minutes
Elevation gain: 250 feet
Difficulty: Easy, with some difficult stretches
Topo: Hollywood
Thomas Bros map: Page 50, section E1
Other family activities: Park with playground, nature trail, stream, pond.

Often when viewed from the San Gabriels, the Baldwin Hills can be seen rising above the fog or smog and can be mistaken for Palos Verdes. But it was Baldwin Hills, not Palos Verdes, that was the site of the Olympic Village for the 1932 Olympics. Except for that claim to fame, it has always been known as a dreary oilfield through which you quickly pass when you use La Cienega Blvd. to avoid congested freeways on your way to and from the airport. But that is changing. The oil wells are drying up, and in 1985 the state began buying up land and soon opened the Baldwin Hills State Recreation Area. Then the authorities decided to honor a long-time county supervisor, and it is now called Kenneth Hahn State Recreation Area. Eventually the state plans to acquire 1300 acres in this area.

The start of the trip is reached from La Cienega Blvd. by turning east, into the well-signed entrance into the park.

From the main park road, turn left into the Olympic Forest area. You park in the 260-foot (elevation) lot and head up the road closed

off by a chain and signed FOR OFFICIAL VEHICLES ONLY. At mile
0.10, with the covered observation platform above you and straight
ahead, you go right, uphill. This very short but steep climb levels off
at mile 0.16. At the ridge you go left, to reach the 460-foot sheltered
bench at mile 0.23. This is signed PINE GROVE, but I'm not sure why,
because no pine trees of any age are apparent. Nevertheless, it offers
great views of the Los Angeles area.

From here, follow the trail east toward two more shelters. From
the third shelter, at 490 feet at mile 0.39, after 10 minutes, you are
presented with a view of Santa Monica Bay, the Santa Monica
Mountains, the Hollywood Hills with the HOLLYWOOD sign, and
downtown Los Angeles, with the San Gabriels in the background.

Backtrack to the parking lot, reaching the start at mile 0.72 after
20 minutes.

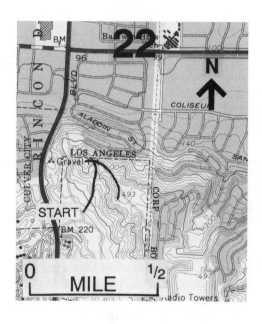

Trip 23

Walnut Canyon

Distance: 7.90 miles
Time: 1¾ hours
Elevation gain: 350 feet
Difficulty: Easy, with some hills
Topo: San Dimas
Thomas Bros map: Page 89, section E4

Once while descending Santiago Peak in the summer, another cyclist told me of a ride near San Dimas that had 18 stream crossings in 5 miles. I thought he was suffering from the same heat and dehydration that I was, and assumed he was wrong. When I think of San Dimas, the words "hot" and "dry," not "cool" and "wet," come to mind. How could there be enough water there to create a stream crossing, any time of the year, except after a storm?

Puddingstone Dam provides the answer. When this dam was built in 1928 as a flood-control measure, it meant that a year-round water supply would be available for Walnut Creek. And luckily for hikers, equestrians, and now mountain cyclists, the floor-control people allowed the creek below the dam to remain in its natural state for the first 3½ miles.

The 860-foot trailhead is on San Dimas Avenue just south of where it passes under the 210 Fwy. Park on the side of the road by the WALNUT CREEK COUNTY PARK sign.

There are two other interesting signs. One, which can also be found in Bonelli Park, across the freeway, gives you an idea of the wilderness nature of this ride, for it reads:

Warning

Mountain lion has been observed in this area.
It is required that children be accompanied by an adult.
Report all sightings to headquarters.
714-599-8411

The other sign lets you know that you are still in an urban environment: USE OF PAINT GUNS PROHIBITED.

You immediately begin a steep descent that takes you quickly to the 700-foot bottom of the small canyon that contains Walnut Creek. Now at mile 0.29 you are riding right next to the year-round stream, which makes this canyon quite lush with many oaks, walnuts, and, unfortunately, poison oak in abundance.

At mile 0.40 you make the first of the many stream crossings, and at mile 0.73 you cross the first of two bridges and pass the edge of the campus of Pacific Coast Bible College. At mile 0.98 you cross a paved road, ford the stream again, and pass through an equestrian staging area and then continue on the dirt trail, making several more stream crossings before you bear right at 1.39 miles.

At 1.55 and 1.70 miles you pass picnic areas, and at mile 2.00 you reach an equestrian staging area complete with port-a-potty. At 2.13 miles you come to a fork in the road. Either branch is satisfactory. You make a few more stream crossings, then make a right turn at 2.49 miles and a left turn after a stream crossing at 2.55 miles.

At 2.65 miles, you don't cross the stream but ride right down the middle of it as you pass beneath a bridge. At 2.89 miles you cross a second bridge and arrive at yet another picnic area. The horse set must eat a lot.

You make a few more stream crossings, until at mile 3.07 you ride down the middle of the stream for nearly ¼ mile. At 3.30 miles you say good bye to the streambed, and climb up onto a dirt path on the left bank of the flood-control channel. At an elevation of 529 feet, after one hour and 3.69 miles, you bid farewell to the dirt completely and turn left onto paved, unsigned Covina Hills road.

Climb along this road, passing many beautiful older, rural homes until you turn left onto Via Verde at 5.57 miles. Via Verde descends past some modern homes and then climbs until it reaches 1050-foot San Dimas Avenue at 7.00 miles. Here you turn left and descend until you return to the start at 7.90 miles after 1¾ hours.

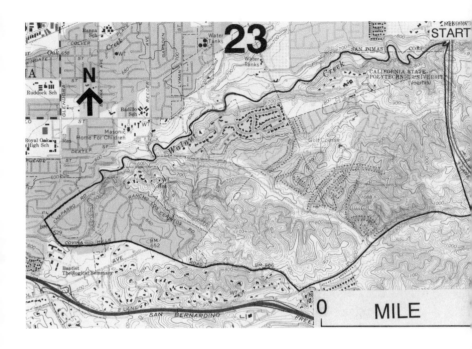

Trip 24

Bonelli Park

Distance: 9.52 miles
Time: 2½ hours
Elevation gain: 500 feet
Difficulty: Moderate
Topo: San Dimas
Thomas Bros map: Page 89, section F6
Other family activities: Playgrounds, boating, swimming, Raging Waters.

In 1928 the Los Angeles Flood Control District built Puddingstone Dam. Its 250-acre lake immediately attracted the attention of fishermen, boaters, and swimmers. In the 1950s the State started to buy acreage surrounding the lake and named the area Puddingstone Reservoir State Park. In the 1970s the County took over the operation and renamed it to honor the late County Supervisor Frank G. Bonelli.

Today Bonelli is really two parks: one a wilderness area with miles of peaceful trails, the other a recreation area allowing dragboat races, water skiing, jet skis, Raging Waters (a water-oriented amusement park), permanent RV campgrounds, and even a hot tub rental. A major hotel and restaurant are said to be in the works.

This ride starts, at 1050 feet, from the Cal Trans "Park & Ride" lot at the Via Verde exit of the 210 freeway. From the lot, you cross Via Verde Drive and ride east toward Bonelli Park. Just after crossing the freeway at mile 0.17 you take the signed equestrian trail to the right. Make a 180° turn and follow the equestrian trail north as it crosses under Via Verde at mile 0.24.

Notice the sign:

WARNING

Mountain lion has been observed in this area.
It is required that children be accompanied by an adult.
Report all sightings to headquarters.
714-599-8411

At mile 0.38 and again at mile 0.45 you cross paved roads, but continue riding the trail uphill. The road levels off and from the oak and chaparral-covered slope you have views of Puddingstone Lake, with the San Gabriels in the distance.

At mile 0.79 and again at mile 0.90 you go left. At mile 0.94, a spot where you can hear the traffic from the 210 freeway, you go right. Descend until at 1.29 miles you cross a wooden bridge and begin climbing again. At 1.67 miles you continue up the hill past the equestrian center and a maintenance building with the notice NO HORSES BEYOND THIS POINT.

At mile 1.87 you bear right and at mile 2.11 you go to the right through a fence where there are berry bushes on both sides of the road. At 2.25 miles bear left. As you climb the next stretch, if it's a hot day, keep your eyes closed or you'll see Raging Waters below you and you will be tempted to abandon your hot uphills for a cool downhill.

At 2.50 miles, after 1 hour, you reach a 1020-foot deadend on a plateau with an either magnificent or depressing (depending upon the weather) view of downtown Los Angeles, the entire San Gabriel Valley, the San Gabriels from Mount Wilson to Mount Baldy, Puddingstone Lake, and even the tip of Santiago Peak.

Now turn around and ride back down past Raging Waters until at 2.75 miles you begin climbing up the switchbacks to the left. At 2.92 miles you come to a paved road and head toward the stop sign. Turn left at the stop sign and ride on the paved road across the reservoir. Just before the entrance to Raging Waters you go right at 3.35 miles onto the signed equestrian trail. After carrying your bike over a log barrier, you go uphill and then at 3.45 miles you go downhill through the gates.

At 3.55 miles you arrive at the shoreline of the 250-acre lake, where there are restrooms, water fountains, snack bars, picnic tables and a beach. The 970-foot-elevation beach is posted NO SWIMMING OR WADING, but few seem to obey on a hot day.

You continue counterclockwise around the lake on the paved path until you come to a parking lot. At 4.20 miles, at the northeast corner of the lot, pick up a dirt trail again. At 4.35 miles, you bear right and after crossing the creek that feeds the lake, you turn right at

4.38 miles. At 4.60 miles you leave the brush and again are beside the lake. Signs warn of a hazardous bottom and again prohibit swimming. Here you go left along the airport fencing. At 4.75 miles, at the end of a wooden fence, make a U turn onto the pavement. (Or you can continue straight ahead for ½ mile for a meal at the airport restaurant, Norm's Hangar.)

Now you enter a campground, which appears to have mostly permanent residents. At 4.81 miles you turn right onto a one-way street. (Be careful, because you're technically riding against traffic.) After passing through the campground at 5.07 miles, you go right, onto the road with the sign ROAD CLOSED, and you immediately go through an opening in the fence.

At 5.73 miles you enter another side-of-the-lake area with picnic tables, drinking water, and restrooms. At a junction with the paved road at 5.85 miles, after riding next to some pine trees, go left onto unsigned Fisherman's Drive. Now make a gradual uphill climb and turn right onto Via Verde at 6.69 miles.

Almost immediately, at 6.75 miles, you turn left into a dirt parking area with a westward-facing MOUNTED ASSISTANCE UNIT STAGING AREA sign. You ride through the staging area, climb, and turn left onto a dirt road at 6.82 miles. This road climbs and then drops down and parallels Via Verde. At 7.10 miles you make a sharp right turn and begin climbing away from Via Verde.

At 7.31 miles you reach an 1180-foot spot on the road which offers a nice view of Puddingstone Reservoir, with the San Gabriels in the background. On a crystal-clear day, you can even see downtown Los Angeles. Next you climb and then descend until you come to a 4-way junction near some planted pine trees. You keep riding straight and begin climbing again.

At 7.98 miles, you arrive at a 1200-foot summit from which you can both hear and see the San Bernardino Freeway below you. But on a clear day, you can see from the nearby Chino Hills to distant Santiago Peak.

At 8.02 miles you go left, at 8.19 miles you go right, and at 8.47 miles you go left again following the EQUESTRIAN TRAIL signs, most of which only face the opposite direction. At 8.77 miles, right next to the freeway, you turn right at the junction instead of making the steep climb which is straight ahead. Then at 8.99 miles, just before reaching the pavement, you make a left turn, and after a short climb, you go right again at 9.02 miles.

At 9.31 miles, instead of entering the equestrian tunnel, you veer right towards the RAGING WATERS/BONELLI PARK sign, and at 9.34

miles you turn left onto paved, unsigned Via Verde. Finally, at 9.52
miles, after 2½ hours of riding, you arrive at the start again.

This trip should be considered only an introduction to Bonelli.
South and west of the lake, there are horse and hiking trails heading
off in all directions. And it would seem to be nearly impossible to get
lost.

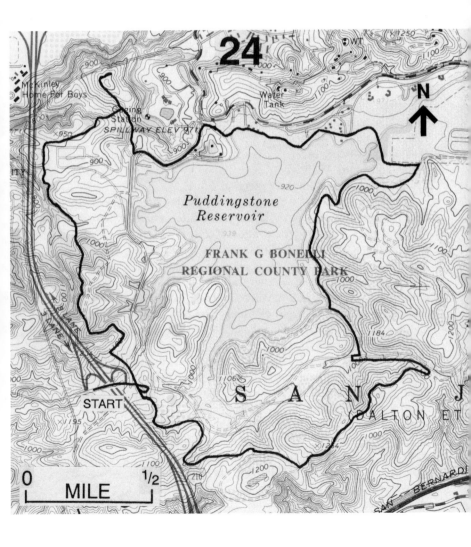

Trip 25

Whittier Loop

Distance: 11.39 miles
Time: 2½ hours
Elevation gain: 1100 feet
Difficulty: Moderate
Topo: El Monte, Whittier
Thomas Bros map: Page 47, section E6

This ride starts from the equestrian-staging area on Workman Mill Road about 100 yards north of the intersection of Workman Mill and Peck Road at an elevation of 240 feet. Do not attempt to park in the Rio Hondo College parking lots. Parking there is by permit only, and no bicycling is allowed on campus.

You ride onto the equestrian trail and down through the underpass which takes you below Workman Mill. After exiting the underpass you immediately begin climbing. The trail forks almost immediately, the right branch being the easier. At the top of the first hill, you bear left at mile 0.22.

This section of the ride has the essence of Los Angeles and is a "must see" for any visitor: the noise of a freeway is on your left, the noise of a shooting range is on your right, and you may be able to smell the nearby landfill.

At mile 0.74 you turn left onto a paved road and at mile 0.90 you pass the Puente Hills Warehouse. At 1.04 miles, after 22 minutes, you crest a hill to find the Rose Hills Cemetery on your right. At 1.33 miles you turn right, following the equestrian sign, which is by the water tank. There's a power plant to your left and usually a line of trucks going up to the Puente Hills landfill. This is the largest dump in Los Angeles County and the second busiest dump in the

U.S. It is limited to "only" 13,200 tons of trash per day. You can usually see a line of trucks waiting to dump their loads. On you right is the Rio Hondo College observatory.

At 1.58 miles you come to a trailside rest area, which has just been constructed. There's no water or shade now, but there may be in 10 years or so, as some young trees have been recently planted. Continue cycling on pavement until you ride onto dirt at 1.68 miles. Beyond the fence to your right is Rose Hills. Obey their no trespassing signs; they are deadly serious.

At mile 2.00 you hit pavement once more and ride on it until at 2.19 miles you reach an 1160-foot summit which, like numerous others in Southern California, has sprouted a forest of antennas. At 2.36 miles, after 1 hour, you reach another equestrian rest area. It has a water trough for horses, but no apparent water supply for humans. On a clear day, you have an excellent view extending from the San Gabriels to the Pacific.

At 2.40 miles, at the east end of the picnic area, pick up the dirt road again. Until now the trail has been easy to see, because of the many horse footprints, but now you begin to see more and more tracks made by mountain bikes and fewer and fewer made by horses. It's downhill, and you get your first view of the result of the 1989 Turnbull Canyon fire. Descend and then continue on the road as it parallels the Rose Hills boundary fence.

You pass some interesting sandstone formations and then at 3.42 miles there is a junction with another equestrian trail, which climbs steeply to the left. You pedal along a ridge above which red-tailed hawks can be seen riding the thermals and updrafts. At 3.86 and at 3.93 miles you come to junctions with other equestrian trails, but you continue parallelling the fence.

At 4.00 miles you turn right and ride through an opening in the fence. As you descend to 740 feet on this single track, you can easily see Turnbull Canyon winding its way up from Whittier. The single track widens to a fireroad, and at 4.72 miles at a gate, you go uphill onto a single track again.

At 5.14 miles, after 2¼ hours of riding, you reach 850-foot Turnbull Canyon Road. Turn right onto it and begin descending. Once you are in the City of Whittier, it becomes Beverly Blvd. At 8.04 miles you come to Pickering Avenue, which has a small market. At 9.19 miles you turn right onto Workman Mill, which takes you past Rose Hills. At 11.24 miles Workman makes a right turn. Immediately after this, at 11.39 miles, after 2½ hours of riding, you turn left into the equestrian-staging-area parking lot.

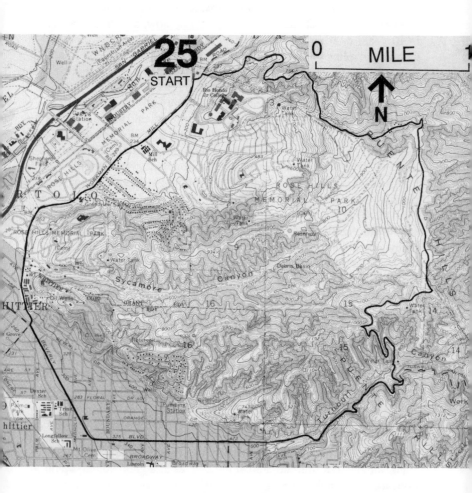

Trip 26

Skyline Trail

Distance: 28.18 miles
Time: 7½ hours
Elevation gain: 2,000 feet
Difficulty: Strenuous
Topo: El Monte, La Habra, Whittier
Thomas Bros map: page 47, section E6

This ride takes the same route as Trip 25, except that when you reach Turnbull Canyon Road, instead of turning right you cross the road and continue uphill on the equestrian trail, which widens into a fireroad at 5.20 miles. At 5.25 miles you go through a spring-loaded gate to the right of the main gate.

At the 1100-foot summit, at 5.46 miles, you take the fireroad to the right. From the ridge at 5.80 miles, with the San Gabriel Valley on your left and Whittier on your right, you look out upon a sea of houses in both directions.

At 6.14 miles you begin a downhill which takes you by a corral and an abandoned motorhome, apparently once used as a residence. Although there are very few horse prints, it's easy to spot the main road, because of the numerous trails left by hikers and cyclists.

At 6.81 miles go to the right onto the single track and through the gate. At 6.92 miles, after 2:40, you come to a huge patch of licorice-smelling and -tasting anise. At the junction at 7.04 miles follow the trail sign and go to your right. At 7.18 miles you come to a paved road, but you cross it and continue on the equestrian trail. This is very steep and may force you to engage your "24-inch gear."

Now there follows a steep descent right behind some new houses. I can see a day coming when this entire ride will be like riding in an alley between houses. Notice the huge, golden-roofed Buddhist temple 1½ miles ahead. At 7.37 miles you cross Holmes Circle and continue on the bridle path.

At 7.78 miles you reach 700-foot Colima Road, which is crossed via an underpass. At 8.13 miles bear left and continue paralleling the powerlines. At 8.59 miles you go left at the power tower with the EQUESTRIAN TRAIL sign and descend on the paved road. Then, at 9.01 miles, after 3½ hours, you reach Hacienda Blvd.

Directly across from you on Hacienda is the Hsi Lai Buddhist Temple. The $15 million structure is the largest Buddhist monastery and temple in the Western Hemisphere. You cross Hacienda by riding through the easily missed equestrian underpass, immediately to your right and next to the CURVED ROAD NEXT 3 MILES sign.

Once across Hacienda, you ride on the single track bridle path that parallels the road.

At 9.77 miles the single track ends, and after crossing a driveway you turn left onto Skyline Drive and follow the equestrian trail sign to the left. At 9.95 miles go straight past a gate with a metal post signed SKYLINE 4.

At a junction at 10.38 miles, under the partial shade of eucalyptus trees, you continue straight. At 11.05 miles, at the power tower near the houses, you go right. Then, at 11.22 miles, just before the paved road, take the trail to the left, cross the paved road and continue on the dirt road.

You immediately turn right at the first gate (the one with an old white sign) at 11.27 miles. This is a very steep hill, which may have to be walked. At 11.46 miles you reach a 1240-foot eucalyptus-tree-shaded summit. From here I thought at first that I could see the checkerboard pattern of some farms, but it turned out to be only the roofs of warehouses.

At 11.94 miles and again at 12.25 miles, bear right. At 12.32 miles carry your bike over the gate. You continue following Skyline Drive, which is now paved. At 14.05 miles, after 6 hours of riding, you have descended to 960 feet and you turn right onto East Road. This is a beautiful paved, rural California road. It has bougainvilleas, avocado groves—one newly planted—horses, and even a realty company called "Country View" Realty. At 16.29 miles you turn left onto Hacienda, and then at 16.41 miles you turn right onto West Road, which eventually becomes Santa Gertrudes Avenue and at 260 feet elevation turns right onto Whittier Blvd. at 19.80 miles.

After it passes beneath some railroad tracks, Whittier veers right.

At 25.25 miles you turn right onto Norwalk, which becomes Workman Mill and takes you past Rose Hills. At 28.16 miles Workman makes a right turn. Immediately after this you turn left into the equestrian staging area at 28.16 miles, after 7½ hours of riding.

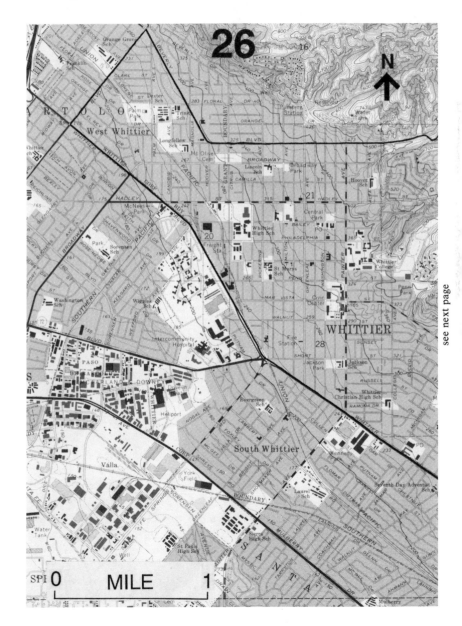

see next page

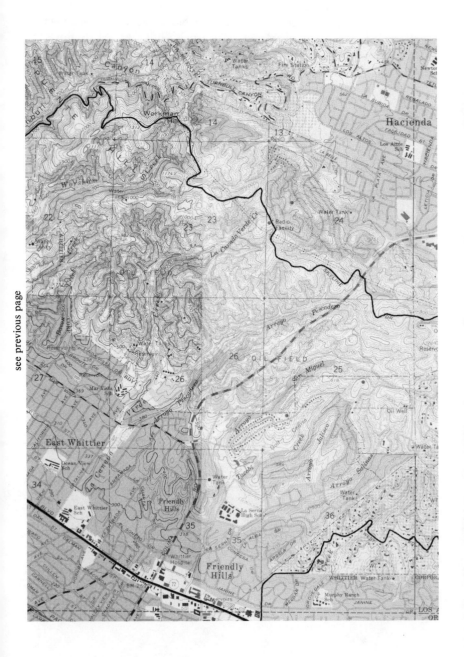

see previous page

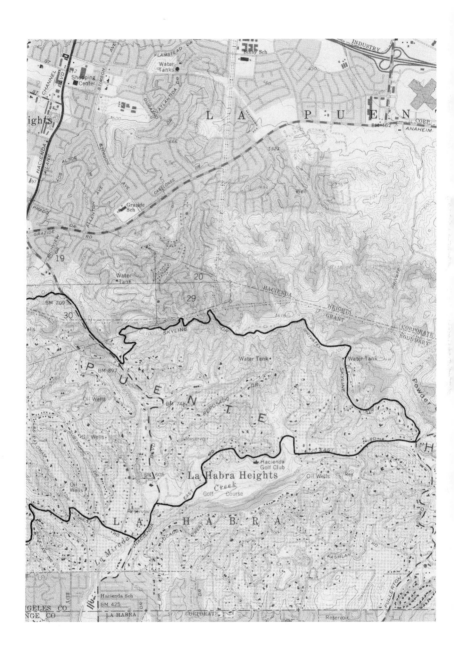

Trip 27

Carbon Canyon

Distance: 2.24 miles
Time: 45 minutes
Elevation gain: 50 feet
Difficulty: Easy
Topo: Yorba Linda
Thomas Bros map: Orange County, page 3, section 5E
Other family activities: Park with playground

This ride begins in 460-foot Carbon Canyon Regional Park, which features a playground, a campground, tennis courts, volleyball courts, and a lake, in which no swimming is allowed.

This area used to be known as Olinda, which in 1899 became the first place "In California to use the technique of drilling with the hole full of water. Having been developed as a source of fuel oil for the Santa Fe railroad, Olinda became a bustling boomtown at the turn of the century. Its demise came with construction of the Carbon Canyon dam in 1959."

There is virtually no legal parking outside of the park, and a $2 fee to park in the lot. The Carbon Canyon Nature Trail begins at the east end of the parking lot, east of the entrance to 124-acre Carbon Canyon Regional Park. You ride through a grove of planted pine trees until at mile 0.08 you follow the NATURE TRAIL sign and descend into the streambed. At mile 0.14 you cross a small bridge, and at mile 0.73 you ride through a "tunnel" that has been cut through the bamboo-like plants.

At mile 0.99, near the #*14* sign, you go left. Then at 1.12 miles, after just 18 minutes of riding, you come to a 15-year-old grove of planted Coast redwoods, at an elevation of 475 feet. Here under the shade of these very thirsty-looking plants are benches and a drinking fountain.

Return the way you came, reaching the parking lot at 2.24 miles after 45 minutes.

By the lake in Carbon Canyon Regional Park

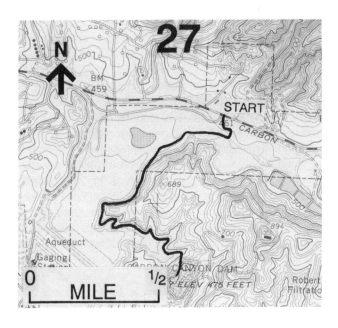

Trip 28

Telegraph Trail

Distance: 17.40 miles
Time: 4 hours
Elevation gain: 1500 feet
Difficulty: Moderate
Topo: Prado Dam, Yorba Linda
Thomas Bros map: San Bernardino County, page 37

In 1841, near the present location of the town of Chino, Isaac Williams built an adobe, on a 22,000-acre rancho. In September 1846 the battle of Chino was fought, in which 50 Americanos were captured by the Californios. The adobe was located on the Southern Immigrant trail, and from 1856 to 1861 it was a Butterfield Stage stop and an inn, famous for its hospitality.

This ride starts from 10,000-acre Chino Hills State Park, whose entrance is extremely difficult to find. From Highway 71 you turn west onto Los Serranos and then immediately go left onto Pomona Rincon Road and then right onto the first unsigned dirt road. Then you turn left onto a dirt road at the sign CHINO HILLS STATE PARK. This road may also be signed PRIVATE PROPERTY NO TRESPASSING, but this is incorrect, as it is the only access into the park for motorized vehicles. If you know that $50 million has been spent on this park, you may expect to find the wilderness equivalent of a Disneyland. But the majority of the money went to purchase the undeveloped ranch property and there are no luxuries. You continue on the main road 1 mile past the entrance station to the trailhead just west of park headquarters, the former Rolling M Ranch.

Start from the 800-foot trailhead. At mile 0.29, where there is a sign to a hikers trail, you continue straight on the dirt fireroad. On this section of the road you climb a steep hill, then descend, then climb another steep hill. Climbing underneath some constantly crackling powerlines, it's one of those uphills that are both steep and slippery. And it forces you not only to stand up, but to constantly balance your weight between the front and rear wheels. Too much weight up front and your rear wheel slips; too much weight in the back, and the bike wants to do a wheelie.

A very difficult hill at mile 1.00 forced me to engage my 24" gear. At 1.33 miles you go right at the road marked by a wooden post with an arrow, and at the 1340-foot Y at 1.89 miles you take the left fork.

Descend until at 2.09 miles you come to an old "Aeromotor" wind-powered pump. There's a water trough for the horses, but no apparent faucet for humans. However, if you look closely, there is a valve next to the pump from which you can not only get a drink but also rinse off your head and face.

At 3.70 miles you go straight. At 4.72 miles there is an apparently restorable 1956 Mercury, which had a bit of difficulty on this road. At 6.39 miles you bear right; then at 6.60 miles you end the gradual descent and ride across a level plain. At 7.15 miles a short section of pavement begins. Then at 7.42 miles you ford a small stream.

After 7.70 miles you emerge from the canyon, bear right, and hear the traffic in Carbon Canyon. Now you're riding through an orange grove, and at 7.82 miles you carry your bike over a gate in a fence and turn left onto a paved road. Soon you are paralleling Carbon Canyon Road. The paved road turns to dirt, and at 8.25 miles, after 2 hours, you turn left and ride into 460-foot Carbon Canyon Regional Park. You can ride around the park's lake and take a break at one of the many lakeside picnic tables.

To return to the start, backtrack via the same route. At 11.20 miles you bear left. The return is an easy climb, done mostly in your middle chainring. At 13.35 miles, after passing some demolished old ranch buildings, you bear left to stay in Telegraph Canyon. At 13.88 miles you bear right, and at 15.35 miles you're at the windmill again. Now the road becomes quite steep, and at 15.56 miles you go straight. At 16.09 miles you again come to the junction with the wooden post and the arrow, where you go left. Be careful of the extremely steep descent at 16.35 miles. Go straight at 17.10 miles, and at 17.40 miles, after 4 hours, you are back at the start.

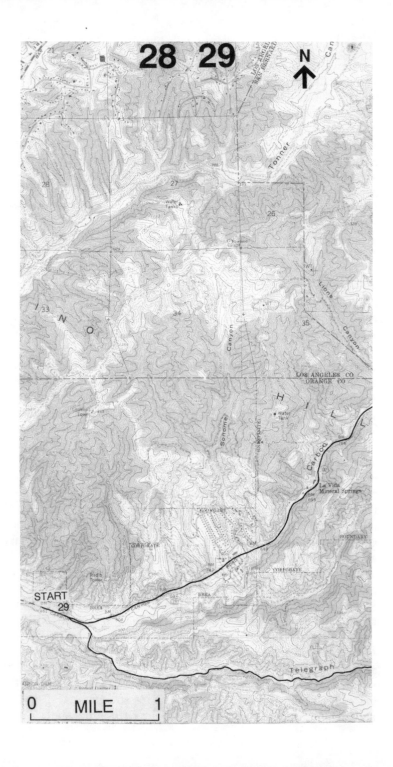

N

START
29

0   MILE   1

see next page

see previous page

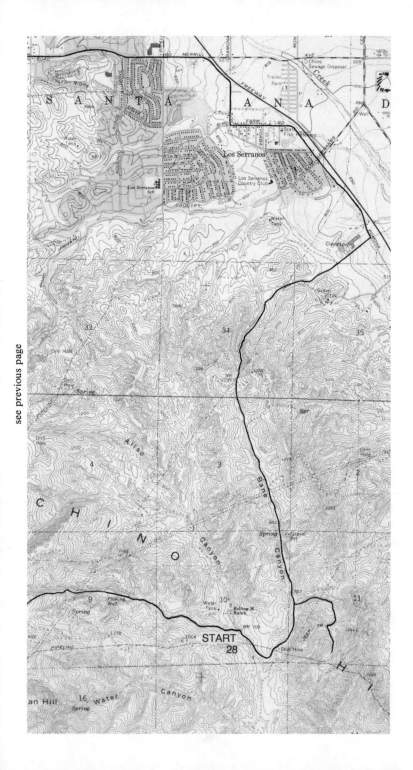

Trip 29

Telegraph Canyon-Carbon Canyon Loop

Distance: 25.20 miles
Time: 3½ hours
Elevation gain: 1700 feet
Difficulty: Moderate
Topo: Prado Dam, Yorba Linda
Thomas Bros map: Orange County, page 3, section 5E
Other family activities: Park with playground

This ride begins in 460-foot Carbon Canyon Regional Park. There is virtually no legal parking outside of the park and a $2 fee to park in the lot. You take the dirt road from the northeast corner of the east parking lot, cross a gate at mile 0.18, and continue on the road, which has become paved and now veers away from Carbon Canyon Road. At mile 0.46 you carry your bike over a gate that marks the boundary of Chino Hills State Park. Here, you take the roughly paved road to the right and begin riding through Telegraph Canyon.

At mile 0.59 you pass a trail register and at mile 0.82 ford a stream. There is a short stretch of pavement at mile 0.96. At 1.85 miles you bear left and begin climbing. This is a very gradual ascent, which for the most part is done in the middle chainring.

You pass some demolished buildings, then at 4.00 miles bear left, and at 4.53 miles bear right. At 5.09 miles you cross the streambed and at 6.00 miles you come to a windmill. Now the road becomes quite steep, climbing to 1340 feet. At 6.21 miles you leave Telegraph Canyon and go straight. At 6.74 miles you turn left at a junction with a wooden post and an arrow. At 7.00 miles you encounter a very steep descent, and then at 7.75 miles you go straight. At 8.05 miles, after 1½ hours, you reach the 800-foot trailhead parking lot in Chino Hills State Park.

At 8.65 miles you pass the turnoff to the former Rolling M Ranch, now the State Park headquarters and visitor center. You pass a windmill and get a good view of Santiago Peak. At 9.05 miles go straight and pass an equestrian staging area. At 9.10 miles turn right at the sign SCENIC OVERLOOK and begin climbing. At 9.90 miles you reach the 1000-foot Martha McLean Overlook, from which you can take in about ½ of the park's 10,000 acres. After enjoying the view, which will soon feature a Panorama Point visitor center, you turn around, and at 10.7 miles you turn right onto the main road again. Pass through the entrance station and then at 13.30 miles turn right onto an unsigned dirt road. At the end of this road, turn left onto Pomona Rincon Road. At the signal at 14.8 miles there is a small market. At 15.50 miles you turn right onto Ramona Avenue. Soon Ramona veers left and becomes Outer Highway 71 Road. At 16.10 miles you turn left onto Chino Hills Parkway (unsigned).

Just ten years ago, Carbon Canyon Road was a little-used country road connecting Orange County with a few sleepy communities in San Bernardino County. However, soaring land prices have caused hundreds of thousands of people to make their homes in San Bernardino County, and now their daily commutes to Orange County jobs have turned still-narrow Carbon Canyon Road into a heavily travelled, major thoroughfare.

At 16.30 miles, at Pipeline Avenue, there are a supermarket and a fast-food restaurant. At 17.40 miles, just before Peyton Drive, is another old windmill on your right. At 17.90 miles a temporary barrier (which may come down at some time in the near future), forces you to turn left onto Carbon Canyon Road. At 19.1 miles you begin climbing, and at 19.8 miles you reach the 1000-foot summit.

At 21.50 miles you come to a small market, and at 21.70 miles cross back into Orange County. At 22.8 miles you reach La Vida Hot Springs, founded in 1883. At 23.30 miles you climb a hill to 750 feet and then drop back to 460 feet, before turning into Carbon Canyon Regional Park, which is reached at 25.20 miles after 3½ hours.

Map on pp. 104–106

Trip 30

Santiago Peak

Distance: 24.28 miles
Time: 6¾ hours
Elevation gain: 3900 feet
Difficulty: Very strenuous
Topo: Corona South, Santiago Peak
Thomas Bros map: Orange County, page 53A, section 1A

In 1769 Don Gaspar de Portola led a small expedition from San Diego to Monterey. One of Portola's men lost his weapon, and because of this, these mountains were called la Sierra de Trabuco (blunderbuss mountain). Santiago Peak is located in what was established in 1893, by President Benjamin Harrison, as the Trabuco Canyon Forest Reserve. Nearby San Jacinto Forest Reserve was created by President Grover Cleveland in 1897. Then, on July 1, 1908, Teddy Roosevelt combined Trabuco with the San Jacinto Forest Reserve and renamed them the Cleveland National Forest in honor of President Cleveland.

As you're driving up Silverado Canyon to the trailhead, you will pass through some extremely narrow, winding roads with old buildings that come right up to the edge of the pavement and you may be thinking, "This reminds me of the Mother Lode country."

In fact this was, and still is, mining country. In the fall of 1877, two Santa Ana men found silver here, and a rush for instant wealth was on. In a matter of days, over 500 claims were staked and a boom camp named Silverado appeared. Then a few years later, farther down the canyon, coal was discovered, and a new boom town,

Carbondale, appeared. Over 1500 people lived in the canyon in the 1880s. It had a hotel, saloons, stores, a post office, and a daily stage to Santa Ana and Los Angeles. By 1881 the silver was beginning to go, and by 1883 the coal also. By 1887 the canyon was deserted.

Park by the 1820-foot monument near the gate at the end of the pavement in Silverado Canyon. Observe the many NO PARKING signs. The surface varies for the first few miles, from bumpy to smooth to paved to dirt. Especially in the summer, this ranks as one of the hardest rides I've ever done. It looks like it would be difficult even in a car. And although old tour guides say the road can be driven by an ordinary car, there is evidence of many accidents: a few cars and trucks over the side, plus broken suspension and brake parts on the road.

At 1.98 miles you may, even in midsummer, ride past standing water. At 3.25 miles the road leaves the streambed and climbs to the right. As you are climbing this section, take a look back up Silverado Canyon to see how wooded it becomes. At 3.61 miles you come to a switchback, at 3200 feet, with an excellent view down the canyon. Unfortunately, this spot is littered with thousands of empty shotgun shells and shell casings and every kind of trash imaginable.

At 3.85 miles you see an impressive peak straight ahead. This is Modjeska Peak, named after actress Helena "Madame" Modjeska. In order to escape repression in the 1870's, Helena, her husband Count Chlapowski, and some other aristocratic Polish artists, fled Poland and purchased land in Orange County. At first, they were unsuccessful at farming, but in 1888, after Madame Modjeska became a famous stage actress, they bought another ranch. Later, after she became Orange County's first celebrity, a nearby canyon and the 5470-foot peak were named in her honor.

At 4.30 miles you ride through some pine trees and at 5.02 miles you pass a stream, which may be barely flowing in summer. At 5.75 miles you turn left at a spot from which you can see above the local mountains either the smog or the San Gabriel Mountains, depending on the day.

At 7.49 miles, after 3½ hours of tough climbing, you come to a three-way junction. Take the road to the right that climbs, not the one that descends and has a gate. At 8.43 miles, the rock wall to the left is crumbling onto the road, which is very slippery and difficult for a short way.

At 8.98 miles, after 4 hours, you see antennas and think "this is the summit," but then you round the 5015-foot corner and surprise . . . you can see the real summit, and have a slight descent and then more climbing in store for you.

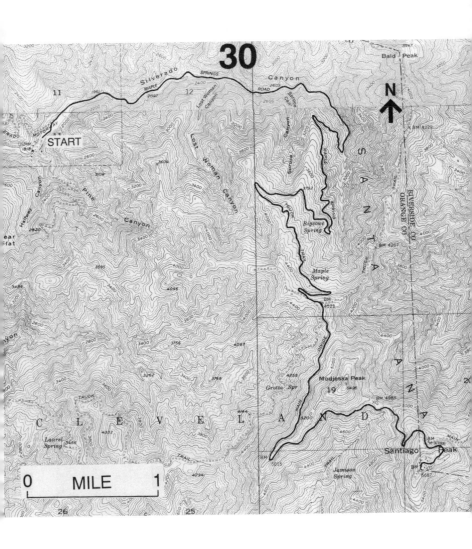

At 10.15 miles, you reach the 4920-foot saddle between Modjeska and Santiago that gave Santiago its former name of Old Saddleback. From here, on many days, you have an excellent view of the San Gabriels with I-15 in the foreground and a splendid view of Santiago and rural Orange County to your right, including several bodies of water.

You also pass a foot trail that was named after a Trabuco Canyon beekeeper who had a dirty mouth and hence was known as "Cussin Jim." But early 20th-century mapmakers, perhaps suffering from a touch of Victorian delicacy, changed his name to Holy Jim.

Finally after 12.14 miles and 5 hours, nearly all uphill, you reach the 5687-foot summit, or what is left of it. It has been bulldozed and infested by more than 175 communication towers. From the summit, on a clear day, you can see from the San Gabriel Mountains to San Gorgonio Peak to the Pacific.

Return by the same route, arriving at the start after 24.28 miles and 6¾ hours of riding.

Cyclists heading up Moro Canyon

Trip 31

Moro Canyon

Distance: 8.87 miles
Time: 2½ hours
Elevation gain: 1500 feet
Difficulty: Moderate
Topo: Laguna Beach
Thomas Bros map: Orange County, page 33A, section A6
Other family activities: Beaches at Crystal Cove State Park

Park in the lot near the Visitor Center of Crystal Cove State Park. In theory, there is a $4 use fee, but I've never found anyone to collect it even on a summer Sunday, and there is no self-pay box. The Visitor Center has restrooms, a small museum, and a drinking fountain. Drink lots of water: even though this ride is right next to the ocean, it can get very hot.

Except in the Santa Monica Mountains, this is the only ride where I've seen lots of other mountain bikes, even on weekdays. Others have compared sections of the local mountains to the Los Angeles freeways. Well, there aren't as many bikes here as there are cars on a freeway, but at least the freeway drivers on either side of the divider all travel in the same direction. Here many cyclists ride on the wrong side, especially on the many blind corners found in Crystal Cove. So many bikes use this park that on some sections the dusty road has only tire tracks: no footprints, no hoof prints, no untouched dirt. It looks like an entirely new geological creation. I wonder what future scientists would think if a section were to become fossilized.

Today, topo maps label this area as the "San Joaquin Hills." Once these hills were a part of the huge Rancho San Joaquin, awarded by the Mexican governor to Jose Sepulveda in 1837 and 1842. For about 10 years, living in the era described by Richard Henry Dana in *Two Years Before the Mast,* Sepulveda raised cattle, and by selling their hides and tallow was able to maintain a wealthy lifestyle.

Then gold was discovered. Miners wanted beef, not hides. At first, Sepulveda became even wealthier, but later, beef prices plummeted, and when his lands were hit by floods and droughts, killing his cattle, he began losing money. Attorney's fees to defend the titles to his property added to Sepulveda's problems.

In 1864 he sold his 48,000 acres for $18,000 to four men, one of whom was James Irvine. In 1876, Irvine paid off the other men and became the sole owner of the Irvine Company. Irvine raised cattle and sheep, leased land to farmers, and eventually passed control of the property to his son. The Irvines resisted Southern Californians' desires to subdivide and develop. But finally public pressure forced the Irvines to sell or donate land for "roads, . . . houses, businesses, a university campus, . . . the towns of Santa Ana and Tustin," and Crystal Cove State Park. Today, much of Orange County is still under Irvine control, a byproduct of this policy being that much of Orange County remains as it was a hundred years ago, including Crystal Cove State Park.

From the Visitor Center, at an elevation of 160 feet, you ride to the south end of the parking lot and turn left onto the trail that goes next to a white propane tank.

You pass a small trailer park. (It would be interesting to see someone try to tow some of these "trailers," especially the two-story wooden one, out onto the highway.) The trail widens to a dirt road and quickly descends to 40 feet, taking you past another trailer park. You begin climbing again, and pass the trail from Emerald Vista at mile 0.61.

Evident here and throughout the park are numerous artichoke thistles. Artichokes were brought here from Europe in the early years of this century as a food crop, although they are a different species from the artichoke which is eaten today. They easily escaped their intended growing areas and began to take over from native species. Although these hills were overgrazed, which left the native grasses weakened, the cattle also inhibited the spread of the thistles by eating them and walking on them. But when the park was created in 1979, grazing ended and the thistles took over. Today, the park is

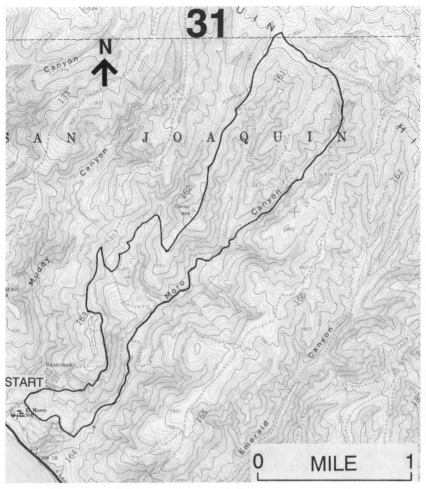

0 MILE 1

attempting to eliminate the thistles and return the area to its natural state as grassland.

At 1.58 miles you go left; then at 2.38 miles you come to a sign DANGER STEEP DOWNGRADE . . . SHARP TURN . . . DISMOUNT AND WALK BICYCLES. This is rather curious because, compared to other spots in the park, the road isn't particularly steep, the turn isn't especially sharp, and a bike can easily be ridden here. In the middle of this turn, you bear right. You see an identical sign at the top of this section, so perhaps it's intended only for downhill riders.

For most of your journey up Moro Canyon, except after a rain, the streambed is dry, water remaining below the surface, with oak, sycamore, and willow trees being evident. But at 2.72 miles the dirt road becomes paved, for a short distance, and you ride into an incredibly lush, almost tropical area, with gorgeous and interesting rock formations sheltered from the sun by many oak trees.

At 2.88 miles, after 39 minutes of climbing, keep to the right, then at 3.10 and at 3.11 miles keep riding straight. At 3.66 miles you see an extremely steep firebreak. You will be relieved to see that you don't have to climb it, but the road does turn left and climbs so steeply that I was forced to push the bike until 3.90 miles.

This area has many exposed rock formations, some of which are part of the road surface on which you ride and are streaked with mountain-bike skid marks. After one hour of riding, at 4.07 miles, you come to a junction. Don't take the fire road that goes to the left and loops around to rejoin the road you've just ridden. To your right is a gate and fence clearly posted NO TRESPASSING by the Irvine Company.

You take the single track that parallels the Irvine fence. From this 960-foot ridge, the high point of the ride, you can see Santiago and Modjeska peaks, the radio towers on nearby Signal Peak, and usually some cattle grazing. In fact, if you can mentally erase the powerlines, this is what these hills probably looked like in Sepulveda's day.

At 4.54 miles you depart from the single track and turn left onto a fireroad. At 4.83 miles you can ride left onto a short single track to see some of the area's caves and unusual rock formations closer up. Some of these rock formations look like they might at one time have been at or below sea level, but others show obvious signs of having been used by Indians as grinding stones.

At 4.99 miles you come to a **Y**. The road to the right leads down into Deer Canyon, which has picnic tables and a toilet, but you go left and descend. The road narrows to a single track and then you begin a steep climb to a point from which you can usually see the ocean. The map at the Visitor Center labels this section "Red-Tail Ridge." Few hawks are evident, but crows and turkey vultures, riding the thermals and updrafts, are everywhere. The single track descends again, but now it is more difficult riding. At 6.34 miles, after almost 2 hours of riding, you turn right onto a dirt road. Descend a little more to 400 feet, and then begin climbing at 6.65 miles. At 7.10 miles you ride uphill to your right; at 7.29 miles go left. With excellent ocean views, the road begins to rollercoaster. When road conditions permit it, really flying down the steep hills gives enough momentum to coast part way up the climbs.

At 7.74 miles you come to a **Y**. Either route takes you back to the Visitor Center. The left way, although it does reach 611 feet, requires less climbing, which may be an advantage if you're tired.

At 8.87 miles, after 2½ hours of riding, you're back at the Visitor Center.

Trip 32

Emerald Vista

Distance: 5.78 miles
Time: 1¾ hours
Elevation gain: 900 feet
Difficulty: Moderate
Topo: Laguna Beach
Thomas Bros map: Orange County, page 33A, section A6

In order to ride to Emerald Vista you leave from the 160-foot Visitor Center and follow the same directions as for Trip 31, until at 1.58 miles you turn right onto another dirt road. This turns into a rather difficult climb that takes you, after 45 minutes of work, to a 720-foot **Y** at 2.75 miles. Here you take the right branch and begin paralleling a fence which marks the boundary between the State Park and Irvine Company property. This is much easier riding. Avoid the turnoff to the right at 3.27 miles, which would take you to a deadend, and keep to the left here and again at a **Y** at 3.43 miles. Now you drop until at 3.73 miles, after nearly an hour of mostly climbing, you arrive at 660-foot Emerald Vista.

Ride out onto the plateau for a great bird's-eye view of the coast. Besides Emerald Bay and the rest of Laguna, on a clear day you can see as far as Point Loma to the south and Palos Verdes to the north, with several channel islands also visible. Even on a hazy day, you can see from Dana Point (named for Richard Henry Dana, author of *Two Years Before the Mast*) to the Huntington Beach pier. Unfortunately, like so many other destinations in this book, Emerald Vista's great view also makes it a great spot for a coastal, line-of-sight, radio-transmission tower, and it's beginning to sprout a few of them.

After you've soaked up the scenery, turn around and ride north, with a little climbing on the same access road. At 4.03 miles you turn left. The road surface varies from paved to gravel to dirt. It's very steep, and the tendency is to let the bike go, but there are sandy patches even on the paved section. The road soon turns to dirt, and at 4.73 miles you come to a trail. Ignore this, as it has been closed by the rangers to let the land heal from years of abuse. But at 4.88 miles, just before the dirt road joins the Pacific Coast Highway, take the single track to the right.

At 5.20 miles, after a great single-track descent, you turn left once again onto the main dirt road. At 5.78 miles, after 1¾ hours, you're back at the Visitor Center.

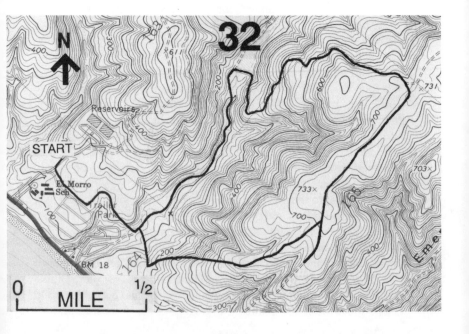

Trip 33

Moro-Emerald Vista Loop

Distance: 9.62 miles
Time: 2¾ hours
Elevation gain: 1,000 feet
Difficulty: Moderate
Topo: Laguna Beach
Thomas Bros map: Orange County, page 33A, section 5A

To start this trip, follow the directions for Trip 31 until at 4.00 miles, after 1 hour of climbing, just before the junction with the fireroad that loops back down Moro Canyon, you turn right onto the single-track, unsigned trail.

You may find this trail a somewhat difficult section. It's hard to keep your balance, and if you fall, there's barbed wire on one side and cactus on the other.

At 4.08 miles you turn away from the fenced perimeter, to the right and onto a fireroad. At 4.12 miles keep on the fireroad as it turns to the left, and at 4.57 miles turn completely away from the fence. From this 960-foot-point you can see the San Gabriels, Modjeska Peak, Santiago Peak, Sand Canyon Reservoir in the distance, most of Moro Canyon and even the ocean.

At 4.67 miles, after 1¼ hours of riding, you pass through a fence with wooden posts and ride out onto a dirt road. It appears that you've left State Park property and wandered out onto Irvine Co. land, but you haven't.

You begin seeing numbered posts along the side of the road. These indicate picnic tables, which must be among the least used in California, because of the few people that get up here. At 5.23 miles you pass one of the two toilets in this area, and may observe turkey vultures gliding nearby on the thermals. At mile 6.10 by posts number 1 and 3, you go left onto a paved but badly eroded road. At 6.56 miles go left at a **Y** and at 7.07 miles and again at 7.22 miles you go straight. At 7.53 miles, after 2 hours of riding, you reach 660-

foot Emerald Vista. Ride out onto the plateau next to the radio antenna for a great bird's-eye view of Laguna. Besides Emerald Bay and the rest of Laguna, on a clear day you can see as far as Point Loma to the south and Palos Verdes to the north, with several channel islands also visible. Even on a hazy day you can see from Dana Point (named for Richard Henry Dana, author of *Two Years Before the Mast*) to the Huntington Beach pier.

After soaking up the view, start back the way you came, and at 7.85 miles turn left onto the gravelly, paved road. At 8.71 miles, after you've ridden almost back to the Pacific Coast Highway, turn right onto a single track. At 9.62 miles, after 2¾ hours of riding, you return to the Visitor Center.

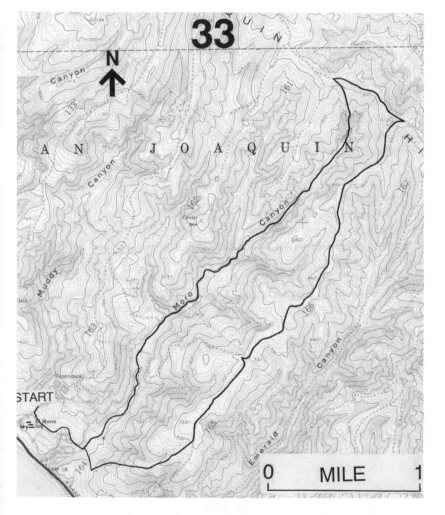

Trip 34

Coastal Loop

Distance: 4.82 miles
Time: 1 hour
Elevation gain: 150 feet
Difficulty: Easy, with one short, steep hill
Topo: Laguna Beach
Thomas Bros map: Orange County, page 33A, section 5A
Other family activities: Beach and tidepools

When I was strictly a road cyclist, I didn't even like to ride along beach bikeways for fear of having a few grains of sand blown onto my bike. Now I think nothing of riding along on the sand, sometimes in the surf, on my mountain bike.

This ride begins from the Reef Point parking lot in Crystal Cove State Park, 100 feet above the surf. The Pacific Coast Highway is posted NO PARKING and it is strictly enforced. There is a $4 fee to park in the state lot, but during winter there is usually no one around to collect it. This ride should be done when there is a low tide. I don't recommend it during the summer, because of the crowds.

You should read the signs at the informational kiosks and then ride down the paved ramp at the south end of the parking lot. At the bottom of the ramp, you will have to walk your bike across the soft sand of the beach until you reach the wetter, hard-packed sand next to the surf.

You head northwest, away from Laguna, and ride along a beautiful, unspoiled section of the California coast, passing numerous tidepools. In theory this stretch is hikable, but the only people you'll see are near the few access points. In fact, except for other mountain bikes, the only other vehicle you'll see is the occasional lifeguard's jeep. But if you are interested in helicopters, there are so many—both military and commercial—flying over this spot, that it's almost like an airshow.

At mile 1.17, after a half-hour of riding, you come to the quaint beach houses of Crystal Cove. I think I could handle living here. At 2.13 miles you carry your bike over some rocks that even the lifeguard's jeep can't get by, and from them you can see a paved ramp directly north of you. At 2.39 miles, after a little more than a half hour, you walk your bike across the beach to the ramp, engage your lowest gear, stand up, and attempt to climb this ramp. It's extremely steep, and slippery from the sand. At the 100-foot top of the ramp, you take the fork to the right. The state is attempting to let this area revegetate, so be sure to stay on the main trails.

At 2.72 miles the road swings to the right and passes some restrooms. At 2.79 miles you enter a parking lot, which you leave to the south and then turn left at the entrance station and then right onto the Pacific Coast Highway. At 3.68 miles you pass the entrance to Crystal Cove and descend to 60 feet, next to a snack bar which has great date shakes. At the end of the guard rail, after the snack bar, you go right onto a dirt trail, which leads onto a dirt road that soon becomes paved. Then at 4.49 miles you come to a bluff from which radio-controlled gliders and kites are frequently flown. From December to March, this is a great spot to watch the annual migration of the California gray whales to and from Mexico. At 4.67 miles you enter the Reef Point parking lot and at 4.82 miles, after an hour of cycling, you're back at the start.

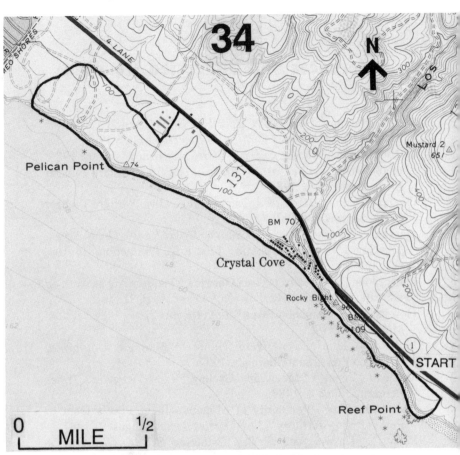

Riding along the beach at Crystal Cove State Park

References and Suggested Reading

Bloom, Naomi. "THE NEW ENVIRONMENTALISTS: Cyclists Fight for Trail Access." *California Bicyclist* March 1988.

Coello, Dennis. "Vicious Cycles." *Sierra* magazine May-June 1989.

Gagnon, Dennis. *Hike Los Angeles. Volume One.* Western Tanager Press, Santa Cruz, 1985.

Gagnon, Dennis. *Hike Los Angeles, Volume Two.* Western Tanager Press, Santa Cruz, 1985.

Hasenauer, Jim. *Mountain Biking The Coast Range: Guide Seven, The Santa Monica Mountains.* Fine Edge Productions, Bishop, CA, 1989.

Hinge, John B. "Already, in Area Garages, Tinkerers Are at Work on a Stealth 10-speed." *Wall Street Journal,* April 11, 1989.

Howels, Bob. "Mountain Bikes." *Los Angeles Times* View section, March 25, 1989.

McKinney, John. *Day Hiker's Guide to Southern California.* Olympus Press, Santa Barbara, 1987.

Milstead, Janey. "Mountain Cycling." *Los Angeles Times Magazine,* June 4, 1989.

Pasternak, Judy. "Popularity of Mountain Bikes Puts a Dent in Parks' Riding Territory." *Los Angeles Times,* August 2, 1987.

Perry, E. Caswell and Shirley Catherine Berger. *Glendale: A Pictorial History.* Donning Co., Norfolk, VA, 1983.

Perry, E. Caswell and Carroll W. Parcher. *Glendale Area History.* Soldado Publishing, Glendale, CA, 1974.

Peterson, Robert H. *Altadena's Golden Years.* Sinclair Printing, Alhambra, CA, 1976.

Schad, Jerry. *Afoot and Afield in Orange County.* Wilderness Press, Berkeley, 1988.

Van der Plas, Rob. *The Mountain Bike Book.* Bicycle Books, San Francisco, 1988.

Well, Ken. *A New Menace Lurks in the Wilds: Supersonic Cyclist. Wall Street Journal,* October 18, 1989.

Index